CASTELESS INDIA

NOT A UTOPIA

WAZIR SINGH POONIA

B.Tech (Textiles), P.G.D.B.A., LL.M.

INDIA • SINGAPORE • MALAYSIA

Notion Press Media Pvt Ltd

No. 50, Chettiyar Agaram Main Road,
Vanagaram, Chennai, Tamil Nadu – 600 095

First Published by Notion Press 2021
Copyright © Wazir Singh Poonia 2021
All Rights Reserved.

ISBN
Hardcase 978-1-68509-621-2
Paperback 978-1-63904-737-6

To

The Memory of

My Late Mother Karamyogini Risalo Devi

1930-2013

The source of my perpetual motivation

CONTENTS

Preface 7

1. Introduction 11

2. Caste and Its Theories 21

3. History of Castes 44

4. The Genesis of Scheduled Castes and Scheduled Tribes... 72

5. Discrimination – A Global Phenomenon 118

6. History of Annihilation of Caste 135

7. Reasons for Annihilation of Caste 152

8. Mechanism of Annihilation of Caste 177

References *201*

PREFACE

One peculiarity which has most affected the three facets of India (social, economic, and political) is the caste system; if any one property is ascribed to which has affected all the three aforesaid areas of an individual in India, it is the caste system; if one feature is singled out which has most damaged and made Hindu religion brotherhood less and missionary less, it is the caste system. And if any system of social stratification which is unwelcome since its origin, continuously being revolted against and still not only continues but adopting more and more virulent form with every passing day for the last more than three thousand years, it is the caste system. The ramifications of the system are many, it has resulted in Buddhism and Sikhism in the form of religions other than Hinduism, and it has caused cruel and forced conversions to Islam by Mughals and enticed conversions by Christianity.

The abler authors and scholars than me have written systematically and comprehensively on this social vice of India. This book is also furthering their attempts to make aware the person about the facts which one must know who is part and parcel of it but with one step is ahead showing a ray of real hope to disband the system. The journey of this book starts with an idea of abolition of caste struck in an evening of April 2015 and a consistent and persistent brainstorming resulted in the possible way of doing away with the system in December 2015 and thereafter it was the physical beginning, earlier it was a mental exercise, and took more than six years to be in the form of a book, in which, the Covid-19 was the most productive.

This book delineates the constitutional mandate for the egalitarian society, the origin, and growth of the caste system, the revolt movements against the caste system. The chapter on the genesis of Scheduled Castes and Scheduled Tribes describes the origin and development of these two depressed classes. The chapter on reasons for annihilations of caste elaborately explains the inevitability of abolition of the caste. Discrimination against work and descent is not only the problem faced by India but it is Global, one chapter of Discrimination – a global perspective details the social stratification and discrimination in other parts of the world other than India. The last chapter Mechanism of Annihilation of Caste system shows a possible path to move on to achieve the objective of an egalitarian society. This book may not satisfy the appetite of literary fora, but for whom it is written, shall understand it, for whose benefit it is, are expected to gain that benefit.

In the last, it will be unwise if I do not acknowledge the authors, scholars, and researchers, whether dead or alive, whether referred or not, whether or not whose contributions find in word form in this book, and if find a place and inadvertently remains disengaged, may be placed in the next edition if comes to knowledge, whose knowledge and contributions in print and electronic form illuminated me to shape my vision in the form of a book. I believe that the creator immerses himself into his work completely to transform the conceptual form into textual form. Therefore he must not only be credited for his work but must be respected also and so I do. I honestly honour the inspiration which I received from Dr. B. R. Ambedkar once I started reading him. I am also thankful to my wife Neelam who encouraged me at every moment when I felt discouraged and disgusted several times, which is a natural consequence, in the long span of more than six years, and the support of my all family members without whose support it would not have been a reality.

– W.S.Poonia

Date: 15/08/2021

Place: Chennai

CHAPTER ONE
INTRODUCTION

1.1

All societies in the world are socially stratified and India is also no exception. But the caste-based social stratification system is unparalleled, which is based on the unequal degradation in which the upper is revered and lower is despised. The Indian caste system has acquired a monstrous state. This abominable state of social stratification is not from its origin, which initially was a class system based on occupation and had mobility. Subsequently, it got polluted with graded inequality and immobility which was never welcomed and accepted. Nevertheless, India had a time during the Maurya period when the caste was destroyed but again with the end of the Maurya dynasty, not only the caste system revived but with a more dangerous form. Some saints, social reformers revolted against it, and attempts were made to kill this monstrous but failed to dismantle it, which resulted in the birth of Buddhism, and Sikhism from the Hindu religion. Social oppression, enmity, and vulnerable scheduled castes and scheduled tribes still are attractions of conversions to Islam and Christianity.

Castes are the building blocks of Hindu social structure. All sorts of virtue and evils have been attributed to the caste system by social historians. In his contemporary philosophy, Prof. A.R. Wadia has observed," The high metaphysics of Upanishads and ethics of the Gita have been reduced to mere words by the tyranny of caste. Emphasising the unity of the whole world, animate or inanimate, India has yet fostered a social system that has divided her children into watertight compartments, divided them from one another, generation to generation, for endless centuries.

The real triumph of the caste system lies not in upholding the supremacy of the Brahmins but in conditioning the consciousness of the lower castes in accepting their inferior status in the ritual hierarchy as a part of the natural order of things. In India caste system has endured for over 3000 years and even today there appear no symptoms of early demise. No social institution containing so large an element of inequality and discrimination towards the majority of the people can survive that long in a purely social context. It was through an elaborate, complex, and subtle scheme of scriptures mythology, and ritual that Brahmanism succeeded in investing the caste system with a moral authority that has been seldom effectively challenged even by the most ardent social reformers. Religion and mythology were used to weave this magic web.

Mythology and scriptures were pressed into services to establish the inherent superiority of the Brahmin and the low social ranking of the Shudras. For instance, Tulsidas states in his *Ramayana*:

"Venerate a Brahmin even if he is devoid of all virtue, but not a Shudra even if he is packed with virtue and knowledge."

1.2

Thirty years ago the constitutional bench of nine judges of the Supreme Court had vibrantly agitated the question of an egalitarian society in Indira Sawhney case, popularly known as Mandal case, on implementation of the Mandal Commission Report. The intent of the Government on implementation of the Mandal commission had always been perceived as a political motive against the core issue of social reform. With the same intention for taking political mileage, the Government and the political class having vested interests in achieving their political objectives read only the operative part instead of the detailed judgement in totality, which, is an eye-opening and mind-blowing judgement on the Indian social stratification system in general and on Hinduism in particular. The gravity of the judgement can itself be felt from the first word of the judgement with which it started *Equality of Status*. Interpreting the constitutional provisions the Supreme Court upholds the basic structure of the constitution for securing social justice, economic justice, and political justice as well as equality of status and equality of opportunity. Our founding fathers had dreamed of the establishment of an egalitarian society through the basic structure of our constitution. And what our apex court observed on fulfilment of these objectives, "That after forty-two years advent of the constitution (now it is seventy years), that with a broken heart, one has to answer these questions in negative". We all are happy and satisfied to read the operative part of the judgement which is the smallest of the small significance as compared to the real core issue and soul of the judgement which no one dared to take pain ever to find out. I have never heard from any legislature raising the issue of an egalitarian society in any legislative house of the country or otherwise on any public forum which is the cruelty with our oppressed and despised classes of scheduled castes and scheduled tribes. In the words of Dr. B. R. Ambedkar – equality in treatment to one another is better than equal distribution of property and resources. Property and resources can be earned by individuals with their capabilities (mental effort, hard work, etc.) but equality in treatment can be given by everyone and that is the idealistic position of social order.

1.3

Mahatma Gandhi wrote in Harijan on 18th July 1935 that Christian missionaries provide education and health with the motive of religious conversions. Dr. B.R. Ambedkar also supported Gandhi Ji and wanted Christian missionaries to stop their work[1]. For anyone, it is a painful act in one's life to renunciate his faith and belief. When and why one will do so? Only when one finds it unbearable and continuation within it, is to live a life like a life to live in hell and abandoning is the only alternative left even for the mere survival with dignity. Dr. B. R. Ambedkar renouncing the Hindu religion and converting to Buddhism on 14th October 1956 is a glaring example of it.

It was an anguishing moment for him when he abdicated Hindu religion and for it he waited for more than twenty years after the announcement of his will to renounce Hinduism on 13th October 1935, saying, "It is unfortunate that I was born with a stigma of untouchable Hindu, which is not my fault, but I will not die as a Hindu which is in my power." For such a long time he struggled to dismantle the draconian system of graded inequality in Hindu society and establishing an egalitarian society

---

1   Hardyanaryan Dixit, Dainik Jagran 20th September, 2020

based on equality, liberty, and fraternity and when he could not succeed in it, but determined to abolish the caste system, he, as a Chairman of the Drafting Committee of the Constituent Assembly, laid the solid foundation for the establishment of the egalitarian society in the constitution with the hope that one day a solid high rise building of casteless society shall be constructed by the future generations.

Not only that egalitarian society is the goal to be achieved but this goal has been associated with the basic structure of our constitution as spelt by the preamble. Our founding fathers not only dreamed of an egalitarian society but envisaged the methodology of achieving it in Part IV, Directive Principles of State Policy in our constitution.

Constitutional provisions enabled the Government to enact innumerable legislations for the welfare of the scheduled castes and scheduled tribes. Recently, in the last seventy years, a discernible transformation in political and economic conditions of these depressed classes has taken place and a separate prosperous and elite class among scheduled castes and scheduled tribes has developed due to improvement in their political and economic status. But despite them being in the upper-class, in terms of political and economic status, the assimilation and intermingling with the upper castes of the same upper-class is a distant dream and still, we find cleavages between these two upper classes only because of the caste system.

1.4

All men and women created by the Almighty are biologically the same, having the same purity of blood. The moment, a child comes out of the mother's womb in the Hindu family and takes its first breath and even before its umbilical cord is cut off, the innocent child is branded, stigmatised, and put in a separate slot according to the caste of parents although the birth of the child of the particular slot is not by choice, but by chance.

The concept of inequality is unknown in the kingdom of God who creates all beings equally, but the creation of the creator has created artificial inequality in the name of castes with selfish motives and vested interests.

Swami Vivekananda, in one of his letters, addressed to his disciples in Madras dated 24th January 1894 has stated thus:

Caste or no caste, creed or no creed – or class or caste, or nation, or institution which bars the power of free thought and action of an individual – even so long as the power does not injure others – is devilish and must go down.

(Vide 'The complete works of Swami Vivekananda Vol. V page 29)

1.5

The caste system in our country is sui-generis to the Hindu religion. The caste system as projected by Manu and accepted by the Hindu society has proved to be the biggest curse for the country. The Chaturvanya – system under the Aryans was more of an occupational order perfecting the division of labour. Thereafter, in the words of Professor Harold A. Gould in his book "The Hindu caste system", the Brahmins sacralised the occupational order, and the occupationalised the sacred order.

Over time, the caste system became the cancer cell of Hindu society.

Before the invasion of the Turks and the establishment of Muslim rule the caste system has brought havoc to the social order. The Kshatriyas being the only fighters, three-fourth of the Hindu society was a mute witness to the plunder of the country by the foreigners. Mahmud Ghazni raided and looted India seventeen times from 1000 AD to 1027 AD. In 1025 AD Mahmud Ghazni raided the famous temple of Somnath. How he plundered the shrine is a matter of history. Thereafter between 1175 AD and 1195 AD Mahmud Ghori invaded India several times. According to historians, one of the causes of the defeat of the Indians at the hands of Turks was the prevalent social conditions especially the caste system of Hindus.

Mr. L. P. Sharma in his book, **Ancient History of India** writes that the prevalent social conditions, the practice of untouchability, and division of society by the caste system among others were the causes of the defeat of Rajputs at the hands of Turks. Mr. Sharma quotes other historians in the following words:

"Dr. K. A. Nizami has also pointed out that the caste system weakened the Rajputs militarily because the responsibility of fighting was left to a particular section of the society i. e. the Kshatriyas. He writes, "The real cause of the defeat of the Indians laid in their social system and their invidious caste distinctions, which rendered the whole military organisation rickety and weak. Caste taboos and in discriminations killed all sense of unity, social or political." Dr. K. S. Lal also writes that "It was very much easy for the Muslims to get traitors from a society

which was so unjustly divided. This was one of the reasons why all important cities of North India were lost to the invader (Mahmud Ghori) within fifteen years." Dr. R. C. Majumdar writes "No public upheaval greets the foreigners, nor are any organised efforts made to stop their progress. Like a paralysed body, the Indian people helplessly look on, while the conquerors march on their corpses."

The Hindus did not learn a lesson from the invasions of the Turks and continued to perpetuate the caste system. In the middle of the fifteenth century, a major part of North India including Delhi came to be occupied by the Afghans of Lodi. Ultimately Babar established the Moghul rule in India in 1526. After the Mughals, the Britishers came and ruled India till 1947.

Our country remained under the shackles of slavery for over one thousand years. The reason for our inability to fight the foreign rule was the social degeneration of India because of the caste system. To rule this country it was not necessary to divide the people, the caste system conveyed the message "Divided we are – come and rule us."

It was only in the latter part of the nineteenth century that the national movement took birth in this country. With the advent of the twentieth century, Mahatma Gandhi, Netaji Subhash Chandra Bose, B.G. Tilak, Lala Laj Pat Roy, and Jawahar Lal Nehru along with other leaders infused national and secular spirit amongst the people of India. For the first time in the history of India caste, creed and religion were forgotten and people came together under one banner to fight British rule. The caste system was thrown to the winds and people from all walks of life marched together under the slogan of 'Quit-India'.

It was not the Kshatriyas alone who were the freedom fighters, the whole of the country fought for freedom. It was the unity and the integrity of the people of India which brought freedom to them after thousand years of slavery. The Constitution of India was drafted in the background of the freedom struggle.

On the same lines of political freedom struggles, the essence of the time is for social freedom, and for that, a 'Quit caste' movement is need of the hour. For political freedom, the Constitution of India is after the political freedom but fortunate we are the Constitution has provisioned for the abolition of caste and establishment of an egalitarian society.

The sooner we redressed all disabilities and wiped out all traces of historical discrimination and stopped identifying classes of citizens by the stereotyped, the stigmatised, and ignominious label of backwardness, the stronger, healthier, and better united we would have emerged as a nation founded on diverse customs, practices, religions, and languages but knitted together by innumerable binding strands of common culture and tradition.

1.6

Secularism is the basic feature of the Indian Constitution. It envisages a cohesive, unified and casteless society. The Constitution has completely obliterated the caste system and has assured equality before the law. Reference to caste under Articles 15(2) and 16 (2) is only to obliterate it. The prohibition on the ground of caste is total; the mandate is that never again in this country caste shall raise its head. The progress of India has been from casteism to egalitarianism-from feudalism to freedom.

The caste system which has been put in the grave by the framers of the Constitution is trying to raise its ugly head in various forms. Caste poses a serious threat to secularism and as a consequence to the integrity of the country. A person who does not learn from the events of history is doomed to suffer again.

The undefined word secular was inducted in the preamble of the Constitution by the forty-second amendment forty-five years ago has since then been misinterpreted by interested groups including a political class for their vested interests and restricted to concerning to religion only, in the same manner, the other undefined word is the minority. We are living in delusion only. The constitutional bench version of secularism is soul-stirring for every Indian and makes him come out of the delusion with which we are happy since this induction. Secularism and casteism are not co-existing; the existence of one excludes the other.

The lesson to us is very loud and clear for the complete dismantling of the caste system and the establishment of a secular and egalitarian society with the trinity of equality, liberty, and fraternity. But before venturing into whether caste can be abolished and how it can be, it becomes not only imperative but inevitable also to devolve into what the caste is its genesis, and development.

CHAPTER TWO

CASTE AND ITS THEORIES

2.1

In early societies, people shared a common social standing. Man is a social animal, by which the societies evolved and transformed into complex form with time from the initial simple form of societies. The complex societies began to elevate some members. This resulted in the hierarchical stratification of all societies all over the world. All societies stratify their members based on an unequal distribution of society's rewards and in which people are arranged hierarchically into layers according to how much society's rewards they possess.

The Indian social stratification is different from other countries due to the remains of the presence of the Indian caste system in addition to other factors seen in other countries like wealth, education, family, etc. People get advantages or disadvantages based on the family in which they are born. Now it is time to delve into what the caste is and how it developed into the present form?

2.2

Definition of Caste

2.2.1

The word caste (derived from the Latin word *Castus*, pure) was used by the Portuguese to explain the stratification of the Indian social system as they believed that classification of the Indian social system was intended to preserve the purity of blood.

The system is such peculiar, complex, and perplexing that no single definition is found which describes its whole spirit, and therefore, we find no unanimity among scholars on the subject.

Senart, a French authority, defines caste as a close corporation, in theory at any rate, rigorously hereditary, equipped with a certain traditional and independent organisation, including a chief and council; meeting on occasions in assemblies of more or less plenary authority, and joining together in the celebration of certain festivals; bound together by common occupation and common customs relating to marriage, food, and ceremonial pollution. Finally, it rules its members by the excessive of a jurisdiction the extent of which is fairly wide but which succeeds in making the authority of the community more felt by the sanction of certain penalties, especially of exclusion, either absolute or revocable.

2.2.2

According to Sir H. Risley, a caste may be defined as a collection of families or groups of families bearing a common name which usually denotes or is associated with a specific occupation, claiming common descent from a mythical ancestor, human or divine, professing to follow the same professional callings and are regarded by those who are competent to give opinions as forming a single homogeneous community. The name generally denotes or is associated with a specific occupation. Caste is almost invariably endogamous in the sense that a member of the large circle, denoted by the common name may not marry outside that circle, but within the circle, there are usually many smaller circles each of which is also endogamous.

2.2.3

Sir, E. A. Gait observes that the main characteristics of a caste are the belief in a common origin held by all the members and the possession of the traditional occupation. It may be defined as an endogamous group or collection of such groups bearing a common name, having the same traditional occupation, claiming descent from the same source, and commonly regarded as forming a single homogeneous community.

2.2.4

Ketkar, in his book, **History of Castes** defines caste as a social group having two characteristics (1) membership is confined to those who are born of members and includes all persons so born. (2) The members are forbidden by inexorable social law to marry outside the group. Each one of such groups has a special name by which it is called. Several of such small aggregates are grouped under a common name, while these larger groups are but subdivisions of groups still larger which have independent names.

2.2.5

Ambedkar, in "Castes in India, a paper he wrote for a Columbia University seminar in 1916, defined caste as an endogamous unit, an enclosed class. On another occasion, he described the system as an ascending scale of reverence and a descending scale of contempt.

2.2.6

In addition to the definitions given by the scholars aforesaid of different fields, the prominent world dictionaries have also given their meaning in Indian and Hindu contexts.

The Oxford English Dictionary Vol.II defines caste as one of the several hereditary classes into which society in India has from time immemorial been divides the members of each caste being socially equal, having the same religious rites, and generally following the same occupation or profession; those of one caste have no social intercourse with those of another, the system or basis of this division among the Hindus.

The Webster Comprehensive Dictionary (Internal Edition) describes the caste as (1) one of the hereditary classes into which the Hindu society is divided among India. (2) The principle of the practice of such division or the position it confers (3) the division of society on artificial grounds.

The Encyclopaedia American gives the meaning as caste is a largely exclusive social class, membership in which is determined by birth and involves particular customary restrictions and privileges. The word derives from the Portuguese *casta*, meaning breeds or race or kind, and was first used to denote the Hindu social system of social distinctions. (2) Hinduism, any of the four divisions, the Brahmin, Kshatriya, Vaishya, and Shudra, into which Hindu society is rigidly divided and each caste is having its privileges and limitations, transferrable by inheritance from one generation to the next (3) any class or group of society sharing common cultural features – pertaining to characteristics by caste; a caste society; a caste system; a caste structure.

As a single definition of caste is incomplete itself and does not explain the true and real meaning of the caste, and therefore it will be appropriate to study the features of caste to understand the true spirit of the Indian caste system. The features of caste may be summarised as hereditary in nature, endogamous in institution of marriage, dividing the society into different segmental groups; having a hierarchical order based on purity and impurity of occupation, the purest being performing of rituals and teaching at the top and cleaning and scavenging, being most impure, at the bottom of the ladder; having restrictions on food, drinking, and smoking; social and religious disabilities and privileges of a few sections and having its conflict resolving mechanism.

2.3

Different Social Stratifications

Universally the society is divided into various religious, ethnic groups, classes, and castes. Indian society rather than Asian society is divided among castes and subcastes which are peculiar to the social stratification, so it becomes imperative, at least in brief, to know what all these divisions are and how they differ from and associate with each other?

2.3.1

Race and Caste

The caste system came into being long after the different races of India had mingled in blood and culture. To hold that distinction of castes are the distinction of race, and to treat different castes as though they were so many different races, is a gross perversion of facts. Race refers to physical differences that groups consider socially significant whereas the caste system is a social division of people of the same race.

Few scholars trace out heredity and eugenics in defence of the caste system. Few would object to it because it was not in accord with the basic principle of eugenics, the improvement of the race by judicious mating. But one fails to understand how the caste system secures judicious mating. The caste system is a negative thing. It merely prohibits persons belonging to different castes from intermarrying. It is not a positive method of selecting which two among a given caste should marry.

And if caste is eugenic in origin one can understand the bar against intermarriage. But what is the purpose of the interdict placed on inter-dining between castes and subcastes? Inter-dinning cannot infect the blood, and therefore cannot be the cause either of the improvement or the determination of the race. The caste system does not embody the eugenics of modern scientists. It is a social system that embodies the arrogance and selfishness of a perverse section of Hindus who were superior enough in social status, to set it in fashion and who had the authority to force it on their inferiors.

2.3.2

Race and Ethnicity

Race and ethnicity do not show up at the genetic level, but the concept of race still forms the human experience. Race and ethnicity are two concepts related to human ancestry. Race is designated as a category of humankind that shares certain distinctive physical traits. The term ethnicity is more broadly defined as large groups of people classed according to common racial, national, and tribal, religious, linguistic, or cultural origin or background. Race is usually associated with biology and linked with physical characteristics such as skin colour or hair texture. Ethnicity is linked with cultural expression and identification. However, both are social constructs used to categorise and seemingly distinct population.

Race is often perceived as something inherent in our biology and therefore inherited across generations. Ethnicity, on the other hand, is typically understood as something we acquire or self-ascribe, based on factors like where we live or the culture we share with others. Race is based on similar physical and biological attributes. Ethnicity is based on cultural expression and place of origin.

2.3.3

Caste and Class

According to Max Weber, caste and class are both status groups. While caste is hereditary with ritual status, class is non-hereditary having production relations. In social class, people have similar socio-economic status whereas caste is of the similar social status of people based on ritualistic legitimation of authority. A class system is exogamous as well endogamous, permits mobility but the caste system is endogamous, and individuals remain in the group in which one is born. Caste is organic and static whereas class is segmented and dynamic. Caste is based on ritualistic or religious myth having non-secular features while the class system is based on an economic, political, and social criterion is secular. In the caste system, there is co-operation and economic dependence among the castes whereas it is missing in the class system. Social classes are based on the principle of achievements of one's efforts but the caste is based on birth. D.N.Majumdar has called the caste system a closed system of stratification.

The caste and class are two distinct social formations but inseparable. All castes have embedded all classes and all classes embed all castes in them. The higher class has more number of higher caste people and a lower number of lower caste whereas the lower class has a lower number of higher caste people but a higher number of lower caste. In the caste system, upper-caste competes with others for the services of the lower caste but in the class system, lower classes compete with each other for the favours of the upper class.

2.3.4

Varna and Jati

A good deal of confusion has arisen out of the indiscriminate use of the word caste to denote both Varna and Jati. Varna is not the same thing as Jati; the former represents the fourfold division of the society and the latter representing the smaller groups existing in society which the authors of the Dharamshashtra seek to drive from one or the other of the four Varnas. Manu distinctly says there are four Varnas; Brahmins, Kshatriyas, Vaishyas, and Shudras while he spoke of fifty Jatis such as Ambhastha, Chandala, Yavana, and Dravida, etc. But even Manu, not to speak of later writers, has confused jati with Varna.

The confusion is because the Brahmin can be called both a Varna and a jati, though many jatis are comprehended under the name Shudra and a group cannot be found today which is known by the name of Shudra. Around the second century BC to the first century AD because of diversified occupation, several occupational groups emerged and came to be known as Jatis. Thus the Varna vyavstha is the textual model or book view of the Indian social system i.e., it is found only in texts. Whereas the Jati is the contextual view or field view of the Indian social system i.e., we find jatis, in reality, today and not varnas. There are only four varnas whereas there are four thousand jatis. One can change one's status with the improved socio-economic conditions but not jati. Thus one should not take varna and jati synonymously but presently caste and jati are synonymous.

Varna is based on the principle of each according to his worth, while caste is based on the principle of each according to his birth. The two are, as distinct as chalk is from cheese.

2.3.5

Caste, Subcaste, and Gotra

The difference between caste and subcaste is a thin line. Both have similar attributes. However, a subcaste is a subdivision of a caste. Brahmin is designated both as a Varna and as a caste. Kanyakubja, Suryupuri, and Gour Brahmin are an example of castes, and shrimali, purohit, and pushkarna Brahmins are examples of subcastes while Bhardwaj, Gautam and Kashyap Brahmin are examples of gotras. Castes and sub-castes are endogamous groups but a gotra is an exogamous group.

2.4

Theories of Origin and Growth of Caste

Like one definition lacks in explaining what the caste is, one theory is insufficient to dig how the caste came into being? The anthropologists, sociologists and historians, and other scholars have propounded various theories on the origin of castes and will continue to be debated for years to come but every theory finally lands in the two common attributes of hierarchical scale or notion of purity and pollution or both. The top of the caste pyramid is considered pure and has plenty of entitlements. The bottom is considered polluted and has no entitlement but plenty of duty. The pollution purity matrix is correlated to an elaborated system of caste-based ancestral occupation.

2.4.1

Traditional Theory

This theory owes its origin to ancient literature. It believes that the origin of the caste system is by divine ordinance. According to the most prevalent belief the four varnas originated from the body of the creator, is described in the Purusha Sukta (90: 12), the cosmic hymn, of the tenth book of Rig-Veda wherein the Brahmins, Kshatriyas, Vaishyas, and Shudras are believed to have been created from the mouth, the arms, the thighs, and the feet respectively of the creator.

The 12th Verse of Hymn is:

"The Brahmana was his mouth, the Rajanya was made his arms; the being called the Vaishya, he was his thighs; the Shudra sprang from his feet."

The later Vedic literature Dharmashastras and Puranas also accepted the idea of the origin of the varnas of Purusha Sukta. Oriental scholars are agreed that the Vedic hymns were composed at dated widely apart from each other. The general opinion is that the Purusha Sukta is one of the latest, belonging to the Brahmana period. Manu not only accepted it but gave authoritative pronouncements on the subject.

Satpatha Brahmana, though later, is considered of equal authority with the Vedas. The Satpatha Brahmana gives the following account of the origin of castes.

"(Uttering) 'bhuh' Prajapati generated this earth, (Uttering) 'bhuvah' he generated the air and (Uttering) 'svah' he generated the sky. Saying 'bhuh' Parajapati generated the Brahmin; saying 'bhuvah' he generated the Kshattra and (saying) 'shuvah' he generated theVis **(II.1.4)**

Tattiriya Brahmana, the treatise gives another account," This entire (universe) has been created by Brahma. Men say that the Vaishya class was produced from Rig-Veda. They say that the Yajur Veda is the womb from which the Kshatriya was born. The Sam Veda is the source from which the Brahmin sprang. **(III.12.9)**

In Shanti Parva of Mahabharta, the account of the origin of caste is different which runs as:" There is no difference of castes: this world-first being created by Brahma entirely Brahmanic became (afterward) separated into castes in consequence of work. Those twice-born men who were fond of sensual pleasures, fiery, irascible, prone to violence, which had forsaken their duty and were redly limbed, fell into the condition of Kshatriyas. Those twice-born who derived their livelihood from kine, who were yellow, who subsisted by agriculture, and who neglected to practise their duties, entered into the state of Vaishyas. Those twice-born who were addicted to mischief and falsehood, who were covetous, who lived by all kinds of work, who were black and had fallen from purity, sank into the condition of Shudras. Being separated from each other by these works, the Brahmins became divided into different castes.

In the same Shanti Parva, the creation of the four castes is ascribed to Krishna.

In chapter IV of **Bhagvat Gita**, the formation of caste is described as: "The Deity said, the fourfold division of caste is created by me according to the apportionment of qualities and duties."

There are many various stories in our religious books contradicting each other regarding the origin of caste.

2.4.2

Manu's Theory

According to Manu, the four original varnas Brahmin, Kshatriya, Vaishya, and Shudra were created from the mouth, arms, thighs, and feet respectively of Brahma and the various castes are the results of mixed marriages between the four original castes. According to him, the four primitive castes, by intermarrying in every possible way, gave rise to sixteen mixed castes, which by continuing their inter-marriages produced the long list of the mixed castes.

According to Max Muller, most of these mixed castes are in reality the professions, trades, and guilds of half-civilised society. They did not wait for mixed marriages before they came into existence. Professions, trades, and handicrafts had grown up without any reference to caste.

Dr. Cronish takes the same view as Professor Max Muller and explains Manu's system. No dependence can be placed on Manu's authority for the origin of these mixed castes. Such people existed in his time and their existence had to be accounted for, and it is always an easier thing for a Hindu author to make fanciful assertions than to adhere to the sober domain of fact, and hence probably the wonderful legends of their origin from certain mixtures of castes.

The object of regulations regarding admixture of castes seems to have been to visit with the females of the twice-born castes and their degradations, and that of their offspring, for unions with inferior or impure castes, and consequently is the origin of mixed castes. Manu assigns to the offspring of the Brahmin woman with Shudras the lowest degradation of all. The whole caste system as it has come down to us bears unmistakable evidence of Brahmanic origin.

Mr. Sherring explains how subdivisions of the castes may have taken place. "The caste separated into clans, each of which managed its affairs, held panchayats or councils, and maintained a distinct and independent existence. As these clans were not amenable to one another or to the caste itself considered as a federal whole, gradually they became jealous of each other's rights and at length, impelled by the national habit of exclusiveness, abandoned one another reciprocally and assumed to themselves all the functions and prerogatives of castes.

2.4.3

Racial Theory on Origin of Caste

The propounder of racial theory on the origin of caste, Risley states, "The clash of cultures and the contact of races resulted in the formation of castes. The Aryans came to India as conquerors because of their better complexion, physical appearance, and build-up of the body in comparison with non-Aryans, the Aryans placed them as a superior race over the non-Aryans. The Aryans got married to non-Aryan women but refused to give their daughters to non-Aryans. The offsprings born out of these marriages were assigned degraded castes. An ardent supporter of this theory Ghurye opined that being civilised and fair in comparison to native Indians, the Vedic Aryans tried to show off their exclusiveness.

As regards, Brahmanic Theory of caste Risley states that the Brahmanic Theory of castes may be nothing more than a modified version of the division of society into four classes -priests, warriors, cultivators, and artisans -which appears in the sacerdotal literature of ancient Persia. It is not suggested that the Iranian legend of four classes formed part of the stock of tradition that the Aryans brought with them into India. Had this been so, the myth relating to their origin would have figured prominently in the Vedas and would not have appeared solely in the Purusha Sukta, which most critics agree in regarding as a modern interpolation.

2.4.4

Senart's Theory

In his opinion caste is the normal development of ancient Aryan institutions which assumed a peculiar form because of the peculiar conditions in India. In 'Caste in India 1930' he traces the origin of caste to the Aryan races. Indians, Greeks, and Romans all are Aryans and their civilisation is the oldest ones. According to him, there are some similarities between the three systems. Like family, gotra, and caste as found in India, in Rome it is gens, curia, and tribes whereas family, pharatria, and phyle are found in Greece. Just as gotra is exogamous in India, gens in Rome and pharatria in Greece also confine their marriages in their groups. Indian Brahmins and Roman Patricians follow the hypergamous rights of marriages.

Just as there is a custom that after marriage woman transfers from her gotra to that of her husband's, the same custom exists in Rome. The Hukka Pani Band custom in India can similarly be compared with the interdict acquiti ignis custom in Rome. Similar to caste panchayats and their head all-powerful man as exists in India; similar councils exist in Rome and Greece. It is not difficult to assign the beginning of the caste system in the shape of Varna divisions to the Indian -Iranian period of history as the fourfold division of society is found both in the Avestan Persia and Rig-Vedic India.

Thus in ancient Persia, there were the Atharvas (priest), Rathaesthas (warriors), Vastriya fashuyants (cultivators), and Huitis (artisans). The only important difference lay concerning the fourth class, which was the artisan class in Persia, and the service or Shudra Class in India.

2.4.5

Occupational Theory

The development of caste based on occupation was propounded by John Nesfield. He emphasised that function and function only is responsible for the origin of caste in India. With functional differentiation there came numerous castes and subcastes. He holds the view that in the beginning there was no rigidity, each individual was free to have an occupation of his choice. But gradually with the rigidity in the system occupational changes came to halt. Castes were identified based on fixed occupation. In his opinion caste originated in India long after the Aryan invaders had been absorbed in the mass of the native people and all racial distinctions between the two sets of people, Aryan and aboriginal had disappeared.

Different occupations grouped from different tribes into guild castes which then borrowed the principle of endogamy and prohibitions of commensality from the customs of the old tribes, solidifying themselves into the isolated units. It maintains that the technical skill of the occupation was passed on hereditary from generation to generation and because of tracing the same occupation over a long period of time, occupational guilds came into existence which later on came to be known to be castes. According to him the hierarchy in the caste system is the result of the feeling of the superiority and inferiority of the occupation. He gives the example of artisans working in metals ranking themselves higher than the basket makers and other primitive callings which do not involve the use of metals.

According to him, before this system priesthood was not the exclusive monopoly of the Brahmins. But later on, when hymn and rituals became more complex, a section of the people got them specialised and became the Brahmins due to the importance of sacrifices such people came to be more respected. After this, the other sections of people also organised themselves for securing privileges.

2.4.6

Tribal Theory of Caste

Tribalism is another important factor in the development of the caste system. Ketkar traces the origin of castes from the early tribe. He believes that castes are developed tribes or converted classes. The aborigines have contributed to the development of castes more than the Aryans. Tribal groups were subdivided into an infinity of tribes that bearing a cruel hatred towards each other, prohibiting intermarriages among the tribes even when their language springs from the same root and only a small arm of a river or a group of hills separate their habitations. This caused the community restrictions and the custom of endogamy. When the Aryans came into India, they also kept themselves socially apart from the tribal, having a superior feeling over the native tribes.

From what we find among the non-Aryanised aborigines of India we can easily believe that the practices of totemistic exogamy, tribal endogamy were particularly strong among the Dravidian and Munde or Austro-Asiatic peoples of India which kept the various tribes as under like so many castes. This feature of social organisation is also observed among the aboriginal tribes of Australia, who are supposed to be somehow related to the Pre-Dravidians of India. Again even before the coming of the Indo-Aryans there had been great cultural differences among the natives of India probably between the civilised Dravidians and the savage Pre-Dravidians, between men who dwelt in towns and forts and had a well-developed political organisation and systematised creeds and men who still dwelt in forests and caves and had not advanced beyond the hunting and fishing stage of culture.

These differences had raised a wall of separation between the two types and each avoided contact with the other. These tribal and cultural divisions of society could not be shaken off by the motives even after their conquest by the Aryans and under the changed circumstances they became hardened into caste divisions. Hence, the curious fact that the caste rules are more rigid among the Dravidians of the South not only between the Brahmins and the non-Brahmins but between the touchable and untouchables more than among the Aryans peoples of Northern India. Thus, the practices of the conquered aborigines contributed as much to the development of caste as the racial class prejudices of the Aryans conquerors.

2.4.7

Brahminical Theory

According to this theory, the caste system originated and developed in India because of Brahmins. According to Abbe Dubois, the caste system is an ingenious device made of Brahmins for Brahmins. Brahmins imposed restrictions on eating, drinking, marriage and social relations, etc. with non-Brahmins to preserve their purity necessary for the sacerdotal functions, they were to perform. At the same time, they gave themselves a high status and special privileges and prerogatives in the Brahmanas and other books and declared all others inferior to them. They said "Whatever a Brahmin says is a social norm and the entire property of the society belongs to Brahmins.

The salvation of individuals and society depends upon the performance of the elaborate rites by the Brahmins; without his ministry, even the King's prayers and offerings were unacceptable to gods. Brahmin even added to the punya (spritualment) of the king because one-sixteenth of the punya accumulated by the purohit (priest) through offerings and sacrifices went to the credit of the ruler of the land.

Ghurye (1961:169) also believes in the role of Brahmins in the origin of caste and supports the Brahmanic Theory. He maintains that the various factors that characterise caste society were the result, in the first instance, of the attempts on the parts of the upholders of the Brahmanic civilisation to exclude the aborigines and the Shudras from religious and social communion with themselves.

2.4.8

Biological Theory

The biological theory claims that all existing things inherit three categories of qualities. Varna means different shades of textures or colour and represents mental temper. There are three Gunas-Sattva, Rajas, and Tamas. Sattva is white, Rajas is Red and Tamas is black. These in a combination of various proportions constitute the group or class of people all over the world with temperamental differentials. Sattva qualities include characteristics related to wisdom, intelligence, honesty, goodness, and other positive qualities. Rajas include qualities such as passion, pride, and vigour. Tamas is considered to acquire qualities that include dullness, stupidity, lack of creativity, and other negative qualities.

People with varying amounts of these inherent qualities end up adopting the appropriate occupation. According to this theory, Brahmins usually inherit the Sattva qualities.

They are serene and self-controlled and possess the quality of austerity. They are considered to have purity, uprightness, and forbearance; Brahmins also have the will to acquire knowledge, wisdom, and faith. The Kshatriyas and Vaishyas inherit Rajas qualities and the Shudras inherit the Tamas qualities. The type of one's actions, the quality of ego, the colour of knowledge, the texture of one's understanding, the temper of fortitude, and the brilliance of one's happiness define Varna.

2.4.9

Evolution Theory

The Evolution theory believed that the caste system did not come into existence all of a sudden at any stipulated time. M.A.Sherring in his book, **Hindu Tribes and Castes** has stated, "The wonderful phenomenon is not a fortuitous event, an ethnological caprice, a monstrous oriental production, the fruit of a tree which grew of spontaneously from neither seed nor root. Nevertheless, caste, as developed in India, is one of the most difficult problems concerning the races of men". It is the result of several social, geographical, political, environmental factors along with a long process of social evolution.

The factors which played a significant role in the development of the caste system in India are Hereditary occupation, the desire of Brahmin to keep themselves pure, the lack of rigid unitary control of the state, the unwillingness of the rulers to enforce a uniform standard of law and customs and their readiness to recognise the varying characteristics of different groups as valid, belief in re-incarnation and the doctrine of Karma, ideas of exclusive family, ancestor worship and the sacramental meal; clash of antagonistic cultures particularly of the Patriarchal and Matriarchal system; clash of races, colour prejudice, and conquest, deliberate economic and administrative policies followed by the various conquerors particularly by the British, geographical isolation of Indian peninsula, static nature of Hindu society. Foreign invasions, rural social structure and Hindu traditional mindset of social exclusion are making large sections of society untouchable and unapproachable.

2.4.10

Ambedkar Theory

In the first place, Dr. B. R. Ambedkar emphasises that no civilised society of today presents more survivals of primitive times than does the Indian society. Its religion is essentially primitive and its tribal code, despite the advance of time and civilisation, operates in all its pristine vigour even today, one of these primitive survivals is the custom of Exogamy. The prevalence of exogamy in the primitive world is a fact too well known to need any explanation. With the growth of history, however, exogamy has lost its efficacy, and accepting the nearest blood-kins, there is usually no social bar restricting the field of marriage. But, regarding the people of India, the law of exogamy is a positive injunction even today. Indian society, still savours of the clan system, even though there are no clans: and thus can be easily seen from the law of matrimony which centres around the principle of exogamy, for it is not that sapindas (blood-kins) cannot marry, but a marriage even between Sagotras (of the same class) is regarded as a sacrilege.

Nothing is therefore more important to remember than the fact that endogamy is foreign to the people of India. The various Gotras of India are and have been exogamous, so are the other groups with the totemic organisation. It is also no exaggeration to say that with the people of India, exogamy is a creed and none dare it infringes it, so much so that, in spite of the endogamy of the castes within them, exogamy is strictly observed and that there are more rigorous penalties for violating exogamy than there are for violating endogamy. You will, therefore, readily see that with exogamy as the rule there could be no caste, for exogamy means fusion.

But we have castes, consequently in the final analysis of the creation of castes, so far as India are concerned, means the super position of endogamy on exogamy. However, in an originally exogamous population, an easy working out of endogamy (which is equivalent to the creation of caste) is a grave problem, and it is in the consideration of the means utilised for the preservation of endogamy against exogamy that we may hope to find the solution of the problem. Thus the superimposition of endogamy on exogamy means the creation of caste.

On the other hand, Dr. B. R. Ambedkar recalls at the outset that the Hindu society, in common with other societies, was composed of classes and the earliest known are (i) the Brahmins or the priestly class (ii) the Kshatriya or the military class (iii) the Vaishya or the merchant class, and (iv) the Shudra as the artisan or the menial class. Particular attention has to be paid to the fact that this was essentially a class system, in which individuals, when qualified, could change their class and therefore the classes changed their personnel: at some times in the history of Hindus, the priestly class socially distanced itself for the rest of the body of the people and through a closed-door policy became a caste by itself.

The other classes being subject to the law of the social division of labour underwent differentiation, some into large others into the very minute, groups. The Vaishya and Shudra classes were the original inchoate plasm, which formed the sources of the numerous caste of today. As the military occupation does not very easily lend itself to a very minute – subdivision, the Kshatriya class could have differentiated into soldiers and administrators.

The subdivision of a society is quite natural. But the unnatural thing about these subdivisions is that they lost the open-door character of the class system and have become self-enclosed units called castes. The question is "were they compelled to close their doors and become endogamous, or did they close them of their own accord? Dr. B. R. Ambedkar submits that there is a double line of the answer! Some closed the doors: others found it closed against them.

As every effect has a cause, we may assume that the extensive disintegration of the Hindu family which we now behold may be sufficiently accounted for. Many theories have been started to account for its origin and its earliest history is clouded in uncertainty and conjectures yet, in the intricacies, inconsistencies, and singularities of its progress and its elaboration in India until its arrival at its present wild grotesqueness is much more perplexing and exciting.

CHAPTER THREE
HISTORY OF CASTES

3.1

Like all other societies of the world, Indian society also has its stratification, of course, different in nature, act, and conduct from others, popularly known as the caste system and is one of the most difficult problems respecting humanity. The caste system as it exists today is neither from the beginning nor germinated at any particular point of time spontaneously in history or being a fortuitous event. It has acquired its present monstrous form through a journey of thousands of years and several different periods of history. But before taking the voyage of the developmental history of the caste system in India, it becomes imperative to study the development of social stratification in society.

Initially, in the early societies, people shared a common standing. With time, the societies turned into complex forms, some people got elevated resulting in the birth of the stratified societies, being the consequences of unequal distribution of the society's resources. The people were arranged hierarchically into the layers according to the possession of the society's resources. The origin of the social stratification in society is the natural consequence and is traced to the development of society.

The general welfare of the first generation societies, hunting and gathering societies, where the men hunted for meat and women gathered edible plants, depended upon all members sharing what they had and having equal social standing with little stratification.

The emergence of next generation, horticultural and pastoral societies led the social inequality. In horticultural societies, people cultivated plants for growing food, and in pastoral societies animals were domesticated. The productions were not only sufficient for their mere survival but more than the needs of the producer. The agricultural societies grew larger which led to the division of labour, and the job specialisation resulted in stratification. During this phase, people started valuing certain jobs respecting higher than others. Manual labour was regarded as less than an actual agricultural job.

The surplus production resulted in the generation of another class of people who can accumulate the surplus and distribute it to the others who need it, developing the trading people. Those who accumulated more than others gained prestige in society. The people started accumulating and transferring wealth to their future generation during this phase. The growing needs of the societies led to the development of different specialised jobs and services. The further development of industrial societies added new classes such as factory owners, skilled workers, specialised services, and wage earners. The gap between the haves and have nots got widened.

The Indian social stratification is different from other societies of the world because of the caste system in India since the Vedic period based on the different attributes. To study caste historically, Indian history may be divided into six periods, and discussing the caste accordingly will not be inappropriate.

3.2

Ancient period (4000 BC–700 AD)

The ancient period comprises the Vedic, Brahminical, Maurya, and post-Maurya periods. The scholars broadly have two divergent views on the caste system in the early Rig-Vedic period. According to one there existed caste system at that time comprising Brahmin, Kshatriya, and Vaishya as three castes, whereas the other does not recognise the three as castes but varna which is flexible in mobility according to one's calling and the attribution to hereditary was not ascribed. But both views are in agreement of having only three divisions of the society of the early Rig-Vedic period and the fourth, the Shudra was created by the Aryans long after the closing of Rig-Veda.

3.2.1

Vedic Period (4000 BC–1000 BC)

3.2.1.1

Indian history in a historical sense begins from the Vedic period which is assumed to have been started from 4000 BC. But as regards the origin of castes there are different opinions of scholars of different fields Viz. historians, archaeologists, anthropologists, ethnologists, sociologists, etc., not only on the timeline but on theories of origin and growth also. Any attempt to discover the origin of the caste system, the most believed begin with the origin of the Chaturvanya in the Indo-Aryan society which is described in the eleventh and twelfth verses of the ninetieth Hymn of the Tenth Mandala of the Rig-Veda – a Hymn, which is known by the famous name of Purusha Sukta, the Magna Carta of the Indian caste system, having sixteen verses, which say:

11. When (the gods) divided Purusha into how many parts did they cut him up? What was his mouth? What arms (had he)? What (two objects) are said (to have been) his thighs and feet?

12. The Brahmana was his mouth, the Rajnya was made his arms; the being called the Vaishya, he was his thighs; the Shudra sprang from his feet.

It is also believed that the division of society into four folds was prevalent even in pre-Vedic times. The scholars believing in this ideology find the basis of the ground of the Aryan race of Iranian and Indian branches remained united till then. In the Iranian society as we find at that time, there were four classes Viz. Atharva, Rathaestha, Vastriya Fshoyant, and Huiti corresponding to Brahmana, Kshatriya, Vaishyas, and Shudra of the Indian society.

From the earliest times of the Rig-Vedic period, the Brahmins initiated imposing superiority over the other three classes of society and also acquired the sacerdotal and ceremonial duties to it. There was a clear distinction between the king and priest and the Vedic king was not awarded the status of priest. But still, till then, the priestly function was not the exclusive prerogative of Brahmin rather performance of priestly and ceremonial functions other than Brahmins is not unknown to Vedic literature. A person other than a Brahmin exercising priestly function can be traced frequently in Vedic literature. Vishvamitra who was a Kshatriya performed priestly functions on several occasions and had been the priest of many kings including the king Sudas. Vishvamitra is also credited as the author of some hymns including the holiest one, Gayatri Hymn. The other persons also of exceptional knowledge and abilities of other classes were used to perform the priestly function.

The Pauranic literature describes Kanvayan Brahmins as the descendants of Kanvas who in turn believed to be the descendants of Ajamidha, the king of the Puru line. Several other Kshatriyas like Vishvamitra were promoted to Brahmin such as Garga who was a descendant of Bharta, Madgala son of Bharmyasva of the Lunar Dynasty, and Harita, the son of Yuvanasa of the Solar Dynasty. There is another instance in Mahabharta (Anushasana) where Gritsamada, who is the author of many hymns of Rig-Veda became Brahmin and many of the Brahmins of today believe them to be descended from him. The composition of a hymn and officiating as the priests were the main two functions of Vedic rishis. The first could not become the exclusive monopoly of Brahmins as the poetical genius was respected by all classes in the society. As long as the making of hymns continued, a person from other classes got promoted to Brahmins.

<h3 align="center">3.2.2.2</h3>

Brahmins in ancient India were shrewd enough and had a strong quest for pretentions and prerogatives and attempted to keep themselves away from the work of governing and could build up their spirited domination unhampered over the other classes including the Kshatriya. In Europe in a wider conflict between the church and the state, led to the defeat of the church whereas in India the struggle never took the shape of the warfare between Brahmins and other castes but remained confined to individuals only like that of Vashishtha and Vishvamitra and

Brahmins were fortunate enough to get the victory in almost in conflicts of the pretentions and prerogatives.

3.2.2.3

Since the earlier times, the Brahmins kept them separated from other classes, presupposing the superior, causing a clear-cut distinction between priestly class and other classes whereas such distinction was lacking among other classes as evident from Rig-Veda. But still, there was a line of distinction between the ruling class and the general people.

The prominence of the Brahmin is established because of the hymn-making, priestly function, and performing of the ceremonial rites. The ruling class Kshatriya is also no less privileged due to its power to rule and possession of abundant wealth. Instead of the continuance of conflict between them, both were in agreement on the principle of give and take so that two combined, one the spiritual power and the other temporal power rule over the common people. Nevertheless, during this period also promotion to Brahmanic class is evident not only of Kshatriya but from Vaishyas also. Promotions of Vatsapari, son of Bhalandana a Vaishya to Brahmin is described in the literature of that time. Vasva and Sankila, the two hymn-maker Vaishyas promoted to Brahmin are found in the Matsya Purana. Two sons of Nabhagarita who was a Vaishya became Brahmins.

The collusion between Brahmin and Kshatriya for the authority and power over the common people resulted in the unity of their respective classes forming their homogeneous groups by virtue of their definite professions and functions. The Vaishyas on the other hand were a unity only by name, formed of a number of different classes with diverse functions with different rules and regulations. Adoption of different guilds and avocations had to follow different guiding principles. The Rig-Vedic society by this time has moved to a more developed society from the primitive stage. In the advanced stage of society, division of labour became a necessity which resulted in different professional classes. The artisan classes in later times were regarded as Shudras, being the mixed castes; all were the respective citizens of the society. At that time no occupation was regarded as degraded, though the position of priest and ruler were awarded the higher status in the society. Even the descendants of great sages adopted the other professions including the artisan occupation.

3.2.2.4

The three classes of Rig-Vedic society, Brahmins, Kshatriya, and Vaishyas had acquired the distinct status and these could not be compared with Dasas and Dasyus. The Rig-Veda describes the term slaves in several places and the wealth of individuals was accounted for the extent of one's ownership of slaves. The slaves were supposed to be the conquered non-Aryans. By the time of the composition of Purusha Sukta, the Indian cosmogony, the slave and Dasas were called Shudras; and hence the Purusha Sukta describes the word Shudra, not the Dasas or slaves whereas Shudra finds no place in Rig-Veda except in Purusha Sukta. The Aryan community became complete with the four Chaturvarna by this time comprising Brahmin, Kshatriya, Vaishya, and Shudra but Shudra was assigned no profession or avocation except to serve the other three classes of the society.

3.2.3

Brahmanic and Epic Period (1000 BC–300 BC)

3.2.3.1

The end of the Rig-Vedic period marks the beginning of the later Vedic age popularly known as the Brahmanic Age. The literature that represents this age includes the Brahmanas and older Upanishads. With the expansion of Vedic Aryans, the society underwent twofold changes, one in the form of development of the society and the second acquiring the rigidity in castes. For making the priestly class exclusive for Brahmins and completely debarring the entry of other classes into it, old hymns were formally set and the composition of new hymns was altogether ceased. The ritualistic rites were also made more complicated so that performance of which require special studies which could be acquired only under the guidance of experts for years.

As the Aryan influence spread over a large portion of land, the slaves and Shudras were adopted as subjects and the policy of extermination was changed. But this led to the social exclusion of Shudras from the other three classes. Also, the earlier notion of purity of blood limited to Shudras and slaves extended even among the different classes of conquerors and it fostered the poisonous spirit among the different classes of the society.

In the East and South, the Aryans found the tribes in savage conditions, having no knowledge of civilisation and standard of living rather their habits were raw and revolting. The earlier conquered Shudras were more civilised than these savage tribes resulting in the formation of another group in the society i.e. the fifth varna having loathsome habits. At this time the question of defilement by touch was raised. The notion of purity of blood further deepened among the classes of the Aryan society between the conquered and conqueror and even among the conquerors resulting in the gradual spread of its infection through all sections of the society causing the rigidity of the caste system particularly in the matters of intermarriage and inter-dining.

Now the number of conquered natives went increasing, resulting in the increased availability of slaves and serfs for all professions requiring manual labour which caused the withdrawal from such professions by the ruling class, which further differentiated socially. As these manual labour and industrial arts fell more and more in the hands of Shudras, the spirit of contempt was generated for such professions. With the inter-mixing of the blood and employment in the industrial professions along with the Shudras, a large number of the Aryan race was degraded in the society which was called the mixed castes. The polygamous character of the Vedic society caused the close association of black women with the higher class of society. Even the marriage between the Brahmin and Shudra woman could not be prevented. The practice of association with the slave woman was common in spite of disliking.

3.2.3.2

Despite the division of the Rig-Vedic society into classes or castes mainly based on occupational character, the homogeneity in the manners and habits was evident in the Aryan community, but later on, special rules were prescribed for every caste separately resulting in the different habits which widened the differences among the different castes even among the community of the Aryan conquerors. These differences among the castes were not the horizontal but vertical and the castes were graded according to occupation. The priestly class was awarded excessive pretensions and prerogatives.

The Brahmin has conferred the status of lord and superior to all castes. The Brahmin was even assigned the position higher than the gods. All castes were duty-bound to regard the Brahmin and insulting a Brahmin would face dire consequences. The priestly function had become the exclusive right of the Brahmin and no else other than Brahmin was permitted to officiate the priestly and sacrificial rites whereas earlier the person with special knowledge and abilities like Vishvamitra were used to perform. The Kshatriyas not only lost the right of performing the priestly function but even the right of appointing and dismissing a (family) purohit was lost. This resulted in the exclusive power of Brahmin in respect of priestly and sacrificial function and it was hopelessly at the mercy of the sacrificing priests.

3.2.3.3

The ruling class in all societies had special abilities not only to the ruling capabilities but were rich literarily also. In the earlier Vedic period many kings were making famous hymns found in the literature, the poems created by the kingly class had acquired a significant place in writings of the period. When the inclusion of new hymns stopped, the priestly class had an exclusive monopoly over the sacerdotal functions and Vedic literature. The Brahmins closed the doors for the other classes particularly the Kshatriya in sacrificial, ritual functions, and religious literature in the name of a prohibition on the inclusion of new hymns. But still, the Kshatriyas kept challenging the Brahmins exclusive monopoly in religious matters and continued competing.

Even well-known Brahmin sages like Balaki, Gargya, Uddalaka Aruni, and Somashushma Satyayajni acknowledge their inferiority and received teachings from kings like Ajatasatru of Kashi, Asvapati of Kekaya, Pravahna jaibali of Panchala, and Janaka of Videha. The Kshatriyas continued efforts and participation in the area which the Brahmins preserving exclusively for them and also found another area, the science of Upanishads where the Kshatriyas were no less competent than Brahmins. King Janaka was challenged by some Brahmins for a debate from which Yajnavalkyas withdrew himself alleging that if we are defeated, it will be said Brahmins have been defeated by a Kshatriya and if we defeat, no one will say that Brahmins have defeated Kshatriya. Several kings attained the status of Rajrishi or king sage.

3.2.3.4

In the later Vedic period, the difference among the castes became wider and wider. As the Aryan domain went on extending, the society became more and more civilised from the tribalism, the difference between the ruling class Kshatriya and the common people, the Vaishya increased and the position of the Vaishyas got lowered. And as the sacerdotal class had already separated it from the common people, instead of uniting together for the formation of a homogeneous society, both the upper classes joined hands to collectively rule the common people through their respective tools of ruling and spirituality and priestly functions. The expanded domain and abundant availability of conquered non –Aryans as slaves resulting in employing in industrial, pasturing, and agricultural works.

This resulted in the contempt for manual labour and the upper classes further lowered the position of the people performing the manual labour including into the industrial establishments. In Satpatha Brahmana it is described that a carpenter's touch is said to have imparted the ceremonial impurity. Similarly, other castes such as Rathakaras, a chariot maker who was a part of the Vaishya class degraded from that position. During this time the professional castes like Rathakaras, Takshan, and Karmara got separated from the Vaishya caste and degraded to the Shudra caste. The next in line, the farmers were separated from the Vaishya community, lowering their position from Vaishya and only the merchant community was called the Vaishya.

3.2.3.5

Still, there was one class of people who were following very primitive professions of hunting and fishing; and living in a very low level cultured and loathsome life. When the Aryan conquerors met these people, finding them much uncultured, developed a spirit of detestation and kept themselves quite separately from this class of people. They were termed as casteless, who were following the pursuits which no upper-class people would like to follow. They belonged to a Pre- Dravidian stock, probably the Munda-Mokhmer race. They were so low cultured and having very dirty habits that they were not absorbed by Dravidians. The Nishadas, Chandalas, etc., originally denoted unclean savage tribes, used to live in hills and forests outside settled habitations. There was a distinction between conquered Dravidians and the Nishadas, and in the Brahmana period, the former was called the Shudras while the latter was called the fifth caste.

The end of the Brahmana period makes the beginning of the Sutra period which runs up to 300 BCE. During the Brahmana period, the castes have attained rigidity and particularly inclusion into the priestly class the door were completely closed but during the Sutra period again promotion from once born to twice-born was not uncommon, rather shreds of evidence are there of entry into the priestly class from the once born. Also, many of the professional castes of the Vaishya community had lost their twice-born status because of accepting the lower grade occupation and shifted to the Shudra category. The Yavanas who were born of Kshatriya fathers and Shudra mothers were accepted full-fledged Kshatriyas if they respect Brahmins and their shastras.

The Sahyadri Khanda of the Skanda Purana mentions how Parsurama created sixty men from the Chita or funeral pyre and consecrated them as Brahmins for the performance of Sraddha. They became the forefathers of the famous Chintapavan Brahmins of Konkan. It is believed that Rama also consecrated several hill-men as Brahmins, whose descendants are now known as Anarvala and Sajodra Brahmins of Gujrat. Similarly, tribes in the remote areas used to become Brahmins by the back door provided some powerful person supports the cause. With the powerful protection, even the priest-sorcerers have been included in the full-fledged Brahmin caste. Every caste had found a place into the Brahmin caste with the support of the chief (Elliot, I.148; Nesfieled P.79)" (Senart).

Thus the degradations of twice-born to Shudra and the outcaste and once-born admission into the twice-born community were prevalent during the Sutra period. Since the beginning of the Brahmana period, special rules had been prescribed for the different castes to make the differences between them as wide and permanent as possible and the occupation of the different castes was fixed. The occupation of the Brahmins was studying and teaching; sacrificing for him and officiating as a priest, and giving and receiving alms. The Kshatriyas were awarded as studying but not teaching, sacrificing for themselves but not officiating as a priest, giving but not receiving alms, governing, and fighting. Those of Vaishya were studying, sacrificing for him, giving alms, cultivating, cattle-breeding, trading, and lending money at interest. The Shudra would have his livelihood by serving the higher castes and practising mechanical arts.

3.2.3.6

By the time of the end of the Sutra period, the society has moved beyond the occupational basis of caste and several new occupations had developed which required some special skills. In case of need for livelihood one was permitted to follow the pursuit of one rank below its caste. Eventually when one adopts the profession of other castes, still he was retaining the rights and privileges of his caste. But when they were claiming extraordinary rights and privileges in typical guilt-spirit, without being able to prevent their abuse by men who had broken away from their respective guilds were threatened of degrading and outcasting but it had little effects. Thus, the Brahmins who were engaged in other professions were looked upon as not honourable, and therefore they were not worthy of sacerdotal and ritual performances however, they do not lose their caste.

It was an evil day for India and the caste system when birth, instead of occupation became the only basis for caste determination. The Brahmins succeeded in organising themselves as an exclusive class. The priesthood became hereditary and inevitably the Brahmins began to pay attention to the purity of the blood and attaining a position of superiority over others. They took conscious effects to organise the social life of the people by writing the Grihasutras (700–300 BC) and Dharmasutras (600–300 BC) etc. The former prescribed the minute details of the duties of man from his birth to burial and the latter dealt with a code of social behaviour and relationships. It may therefore be said that the starting point of the caste system was the later Vedic period age (800-500 BC) and the Epic age (500-200 BC). Since the basis of social stratification was the division of labour, therefore, in its original forms, it was the class system rather than the caste system.

3.2.4

Maurya and Post-Maurya Period (300 BC–700 AD)

During the Sutra period, the occupations had acquired the status of castes, and subsequently, the castes had become birth based. Even on changing the profession for livelihood, the caste would remain unchanged as it was at the time of birth. From 322 BC India got politically united under the rule of Chander Gupt Maurya. Because of the unitary command in the whole of India, the status of equality was promoted. The inequality which existed previously in the society was demolished resulting in the dismantling of the caste system. Various restrictions were removed which were imposed by the Brahmins on Shudras and the supremacy of royal law over the dharam law was enforced. Ashoka promoted the universal brotherhood and further discouraged the caste system in the society and caste could not get the rigidity during this period. The rights and privileges of Brahmin were significantly curtailed which lost their spiritual and ceremonial supremacy.

Sunga dynasty established by Pushymitra Sunga, by killing the last Maurya ruler, ruled India for more than a hundred years upto 72 BC by different Sungas. Pushymitra was an ardent supporter of Brahmanism. Following Sungas, Kanva, and Kushan kings promoted Brahmanic religion vehemently and imposed a large number of severe restrictions on Shudras and imposed the spiritual and ceremonial duties in all events related to people right from birth to death. Manu Smiriti was written during this period whose probable date is believed to be 184 AD. The equality in law was destroyed and the Brahmins give themselves special privileges, established supremacy once again and the caste system was further developed on very rigid lines.

Brahmanism which was restored in the previous regimes got further stimulus during the rule of Guptas which spanned over 300AD to 500 AD. The caste system continued on the hereditary lines but marriage between the castes was found to be prevalent. Shudras in this period were not restricted to only serving the upper-caste but became traders, artisans, and agriculturists yet untouchability existed. The end of Guptas rule resulted in small realms for a considerable time. Again these disintegrated units were brought under one rule during the period of Harsh Vardhana. The caste system continued as it was during the rule of Guptas.

3.3

Medieval Period (700 AD–1757 AD)

3.3.1

The medieval period comprises the Rajput period (700 AD–1200 AD) and the Muslim period (1200 AD–1757 AD). After the death of Harsha Vardhana again the unity of India got disintegrated into small independent units. These small realms were ruled independently by different Rajput rulers. The Indian social system remained static during the period of Rajput rulers rather the caste rules became more stringent and rigidity in the caste system further strengthened.

3.3.2

Rajput Period (700 AD–1200 AD)

The disintegration into small units promoted the different cultures and even the caste rules varied from one unit to another. A large number of new castes and subcastes were formed. Brahmin castes itself were disintegrated into several subcastes and were designated according to the region they belong like Kanaujia Brahmin, Konkan Brahmin, Telugu Brahmin, and so on. Similarly, the Kshatriya and Vaishya castes were further divided into subcastes. These castes and subcastes were self-centric and were concerned with the interests of their own castes. The disintegration into small units and further division of society into castes and subcastes had adverse effects on the social and political system of India. Before the advent of Muslims, our caste system acquired rigidity in terms of mobility and framed stringent rules for each caste.

3.3.3

Muslim Period (1200 AD–1757 AD)

Right from the seventh century, the Muslims were attempting to enter India but in reality, they could succeed in the twelfth century when Mahmud Gori established his rule in 1175 AD and different Muslim rulers ruled the country till 1757 AD. The caste system during the period further became more rigid. Muslims could not be absorbed into the Hindu fold because of the fundamental difference in the worship of polytheism and monotheism. Muslims led a religious crusade on Hindus and forcibly converted Hindus to Islam. Brahmins protected the Hindus from being proselytised. But simultaneously, Brahmins imposed severe restrictions on Hindus making a caste system, a much rigid system.

The Bhakti saints and poets like Ramanuj, Kabir, Nanak, Chaitanya, Tuka Ram, Tulsidas, Namdev etc. preached Bhakti's cult in this period which denounced idolatry and preached the people regarding equality of all people and against the caste system, yet they could not disintegrate the caste system because Brahmins had been very successful in imposing their superiority on Hindus in religious and social matters. The Hindus believing in idolatry worship of gods and goddesses in the temples and temples control being in the hands of Brahmins, helped them undue influencing the common Hindu who followed the stringent rules of castes imposed by Brahmins. The caste system became more complex and rigid during this period.

3.4

British Period (1757 AD–1947 AD)

3.4.1

East India Company and Rise of British Rule Period (1757 AD–1918 AD)

The East India Company arranged a commercial treaty with Mughal emperor Jahangir in 1612 and resultantly established its first trading post in Surat in 1619 and subsequently extended its commercial activities in Madras 1639, Bombay 1668, and Calcutta in 1690. It was during this period that the isolation of India came to end and contacts with other parts of the world were established. By 1774 it conquered India from the Muslim rulers and Marathas and established British rule.

The country had material development during the British period. The administrative and socio-economic policies and legislative measures were taken which brought changes in the caste structure of the society. The disputes which were being resolved by Panchayats earlier were decided by the civil and criminal courts which reduced the authority of the Panchayat. The Caste Disabilities Act of 1850, the Widow Remarriage Act of 1856, and the Special Marriage Act of 1872 had a significant effect on the caste system and social structure of India. Although these measures were taken for the administration, they affected the caste system in weakening some of its attributes. Ghurye (1961:190) also writes that most of the activities of the British Government were dictated by prudence of administration and not with the objective of the abolition of caste.

During this period social reformers like Raja Ram Mohan Roy, K.C.Sen, and D.N. Tagore vehemently opposed the caste barriers. The Brahma Samaj founded by them rejected the worship of idols and sacrificial rituals and promoted brotherhood. Justice Ranade's Prarthna Samaj was instrumental in advocating inter-dinning; intercaste marriage and remarriage of a widow.

The Arya Samaj founded by Swami Dayanand was another social organisation that believed in *One Veda, One Religion, and One God* and rejected the Smritis and Puranas which are full of caste rules and regulations, and raised a strong voice against the caste system. The Samaj started the suddhi movement for the outcastes, the converts, and other externals. Swami Vivekananda preached that the caste system is for those who are away from God and it should be abolished. Vivekananda proclaimed that caste has nothing to do with Hinduism or religion or birth and Hindu culture and civilisation are the most superior.

3.4.2

Period of Freedom Struggle (1919 AD–1947 AD)

3.4.2.1

This period was the most significant in Indian history from the perspective of political awareness, economic development, and solidarity in social classes for the Independence movement. It was the time when Dr. B. R. Ambedkar could succeed in instilling the spirit of self-realisation and injustice done for the centuries to the Shudras to whom he called untouchables. The British made significant changes for the administrative perspective even if some legislation were enacted which affected the social life of India such as The Caste Disabilities Act of 1850. Special Marriage Act 1872. But as such the caste system even during this period continued to flourish. Rather, the responsibility of tax collection was given to higher castes which further strengthened the position of upper castes over the lower castes. The industrialisation of India got started after the Second World War which resulted in the migration of the people from one place to another more prominently from rural to urban regions.

3.4.2.2

After the Second World War industrialisation got the stimulus, the production scale in industries made the commodities cheaper as well as superior in quality which destroyed the old crafts in rural India at a large scale. People became helpless to work in industries for their survival. The industries were based in the urban areas which resulted in the migration of people from the rural area to urban areas. Occupational mobility and movements from the compact ancestral villages started breaking down those caste norms which did not concern marriage. The caste rigidity in rural areas was more severe as compared to the urban population. The movement of people from one place to another on a large scale led to the development of transport facilities like buses and trains. These means of transports of crowded trains and buses resulted in the breaking of ceremonial purity, communal prohibitions. Working at the same place in industrial houses and living in common residences collectively, leaving their families behind in villages, gave a further blow to the untouchability.

These people while visiting their villages to meet their families led to the gradual loosening of caste rigidity in villages also on the lines of urban areas. The social osmosis between rural and urban areas led to the breakup of several caste attributes but still, deep-rooted social customs and marriage relations could not be affected at all. Industrialisation had a strong impact on the caste rigidity and positively encouraged the brotherhood among the co-fellows forming the class society among such groups preferring over the caste society.

3.4.2.3

The transformation of the old crafts society into the industrialised society led to the development of cities. The migration of people from rural to urban for their livelihood changed their notion of division among the people based on the caste lines. The people resided together irrespective of the caste affiliations. The urban population residences were based on class specifics instead of caste specifics. Not only the commensal inhibitions have been relaxed but the authorities of Brahmins have also come to be questioned.

Referring to the M. N. Srinivas (1962:85-86) has stated that due to the migration of Brahmins to towns, the non-Brahmins refused to show the same respect which they showed before and inter-caste eating and drinking taboos are also somewhat weekend. Ghurye (1961-202) also accepted these changes in the rigidities of the caste system due to the growth of the city life with its migratory populations. Kinley Devish (1951) held that the anonymity, congestion, mobility, secularism, and changeability of the city make the operation of caste virtually impossible.

3.5

Post-Independence Period

India got its independence in 1947 and was declared a welfare state through its constitution which came into being on 26th January 1950, known as Republic Day. The framers of our constitution desired to secure justice for all citizens in social, political, and economic spheres. They realised that the inequitable forces embedded in the socio-economic system and political organisation had resulted in deprivation and disadvantages for the poor and the weaker section of the society. So they considered it necessary to provide specific safeguards to scheduled Castes and Scheduled Tribes, who were the most deprived, weak, and vulnerable among the various sections of Indian society.

The pace of industrial and urban development got the boost up after independence which affected the caste system most and additionally enactment of several laws, socio-economic reforms, growth of modern professions, market economy played a crucial role in weakening the caste system. Our constitution provisioned for securing justice, liberty, and equality to all persons irrespective of the difference in caste, creed, or religion, and the abolition of untouchability helped in the dissolution of rigidity of the caste system. Making education in the priority sector resulted in a steep rise in literacy. Education makes people liberal, broad-minded, rational and democratic. Educated people least believe in caste norms.

The modern production systems, new types of professions for livelihood, the adoption of westernisation, increased global communications caused the demolition of taboos against food and water sharing. The notion that a person is defiled by a lower caste man coming in contact with the upper-caste finds no place in the present Indian society particularly the urban society. Nevertheless, the existence of caste pride is a reality in society. Organisations based on caste are being established for securing social and political power. Increased caste feelings are now resulting in caste conflicts. A tug of war already has started among all castes including the upper-caste for securing the reservation of its caste in employment and educational institutions. A reverse trend is being observed that upper castes are competing with lower castes in the matter of reservation in employment and educational institutes.

In the last two centuries, a lot of changes have taken place in the caste system and these changes are more discernible and assertive particularly in the last seventy years. The caste system has covered a voyage of more than 3000 years and several stages have taken place right from the original class system of varna of equality to the most abhorred, despised, and graded inequality to the present monstrous, graded inequality but with some flexibility in some attributes. None of the stages was changed overnight and spontaneous but travelled a long journey from one stage to another. The present state is also neither of the overnight process nor a by-product of any other process but several processes as follows made consequent changes in the caste system.

The one group of processes Sanskritisation, Westernisation, and Modernisation transformed the caste system from rigidity to flexibility in commensal taboos, communication with different castes. Westernisation has affected outlook towards rationality, a quest for material progress and high social mobility; whereas modernisation resulted in mass mobilisation, empathy, belief with perfections, specialisation and super specialisation in work and weakening of rigidity is a natural consequence because of public places like parks, restaurants, canteen hotels, offices and communication systems like buses and trains, etc. where inter-dining and sharing places is inevitable.

3.6

Contemporary India

The last two decades have shown a tremendous improvement in the literacy rate of India. Rationality, analytic power of the mind, understanding capabilities, and a wider horizon of thinking is directly related to education. The consciousness of self-development may also be attributed to education. All these must have contributed to the dissolution of the caste system but we are unfortunate as neither the system is dismantled nor it is appearing that it will happen in near future despite many attributes of the caste system have melted out significantly. Harold Gould (1987: 156) is of opinion that in contemporary urban India, caste persists in the form of complex networks of interest groups while in rural India; it functions as a system of social strata which are hierarchically graded, endogamous, and occupationally and virtually specialised.

Not only the caste system making its grip stronger and stronger, but the change in the attitude of people of different castes in the direction of rising above the other castes and the intent of gaining social prestige is also distinctly evident. The efforts are not in the direction of dissolving the caste system but making the solidarity of caste as paramount important to gain social, political, and economical advantages over the other castes. Electrified by the in-group feeling, they want to hold the caste system all the more tenaciously.

Nevertheless, after independence caste structure has considerably changed. Though two important features of heredity membership and hierarchy have not changed at all. We do find some changes in the endogamy characteristic, a significant change in the characteristics of traditional occupation, in commensal restriction, in the idea of purity and pollution, in restrictions on social relationships, and the powers enjoyed by the caste councils. The most important change we find these days in the caste system is that there has grown a desire among the lower castes to improve their lot and as a consequence, the higher caste keeps on attempting to make them stick to their societal position. This has led to prejudices and conflicts among different castes.

M. N. Srinivas (1952, reprieve 1985) has maintained that the mutual right and obligations among the castes are crumbling down. Loyalty of people is towards their caste instead of their place or religion. Ghurye (1961-209-210) thought that the caste system has shed some of its features. He said "caste no longer rigidly determines an individual's occupation but continues to prescribe almost in its old vigour the circle into which one has to marry. One has still to depend very largely on one's caste for help at a critical period, of one's life, like marriage and death.

Kapadias (*Caste in Transitions* in sociological Bulletin, September 1962:75) tried to study the transitional nature of the different characteristics of the caste system by focusing on four characteristics: caste councils, commensal taboos, ceremonial purity, and endogamy.

Untouchability has completely lost its efficacy in the urban population, the place of working i.e. offices and industrial establishments but to some extent, it is prevalent in rural areas. The rigidity of commensal taboos has decreased a lot and the gravity of ceremonial purity has also declined to a large extent. Inter-caste marriages are increasing at a faster pace in urban society and literate class but it is not unknown to the rural section of the society also. This is another characteristic, endogamy of caste has weakened. Caste-based occupation is no more, except the priesthood and ceremonial rites which are still in the exclusive domain of Brahmins. The Brahmins have occupied every profession and occupation including shoes and wine business but not only priesthood and ceremonial rites are still prohibited for other castes, but even the Scheduled Castes and Scheduled Tribes are also denied to worship in the temples despite believing all are equal before God.

Harold Gould holds that the feature of the adaptive structure of caste in India is evident not only in the cities but in the villages too where the caste system continues to perform functions of security, solidarity, and preferential treatment to groupings of people. For the last two or three decades, the associations on the caste lines are on the increase. Even if the associations are class-based, still caste-based association within the class-based association nowadays is common. The students' associations are class-based but within that, we find caste-based associations.

Different classes of the society are disintegrated vertically on caste lines distinctly. The employees' associations and professional associations are formed on caste lines. Even the professional associations which are formed purely on a class basis, the voting pattern in the elections of the executive bodies of such associations is dominantly held on caste lines ignoring the merit of candidates. Not only that where the organisations are caste-based, the voting pattern in the election of their executive is gotra based, it is not exaggerated but the reality of society.

Our constitution envisages the establishment of an egalitarian society and legislative bodies are empowered to enact the laws to that effect. All the legislative bodies of the country are represented by different political parties, resulting in the burden of the constitution of egalitarian society on the shoulders of political parties. Contrary to the mandate of the objective of an egalitarian society, the political parties themselves are encouraging casteism, by forming different caste cells in their organisation, promoting the caste-based functions and programmes, nominating candidates for the election on a caste basis, and finally while forming the government; legislatures are inducted into the ministry on the caste lines. It will not be an exaggeration to draw an inference that the political parties are working contrary to the constitutional mandate of an egalitarian society.

CHAPTER FOUR

THE GENESIS OF SCHEDULED CASTES AND SCHEDULED TRIBES

4.1

Broadly speaking, the depressed classes of the Indian population is divided into two categories, the Scheduled Castes and Scheduled Tribes. The former is a group of castes, connoting the class of the Indian caste system, at the bottom of the caste pyramid, whereas the latter is a group of tribes relating to the aboriginals of India, who are the habitats of forests and hills. The genesis of the Scheduled Caste is found in Shudra and therefore to study who are Scheduled Castes, it becomes essential to know about who Shudras were?

4.2

4.2.1

Any attempt to discover who the Shudras were and how they came to be the fourth Varna must begin with the origin of the Chaturvarna, in the Indo-Aryan society. A study of the Chaturvarna must in its tune starts with a study of the ninetieth Hymn of the Tenth Mandela of the Rig-Veda – a Hymn which is a theory of the origin of the universe. There are sixteen verses in Purusha Sukta which all do not have the same significance and, Verses 11 and 12 (chapter 3) fall into a different category and describe the class of the Indo-Aryan society.

Prima facie these verses do no more than explain, how the four classes, namely, (i) Brahmins or priests (ii) Kshatriyas or soldiers (iii) Vaishyas or traders, and (iv) Shudras or menials, arose from the body of the creator. The constitution of society prescribed by the Purusha Sukta is known as Chaturvarna. As a divine injunction, it naturally becomes the ideal of the Indo-Aryan society. This ideal of Chaturvarna was the mould in which the life of the Indo-Aryan community in its early or liquid state was cast. It is this mould, which gave the Indo-Aryan community its peculiar shape and structure.

4.2.2

In support of the Purusha Sukta, reference may be made to the Apastamba Dharma Sutra and the Vasishtha Dharma Sutra. Many lawgivers have retreated their sanctity and finally the law laid by Manu, the architect of the Hindu society. For Manu, he did two things; in the first place, he enunciated afresh the ideal of the Purusha Sukta as a part of the divine injunction. He said for the prosperity of the world, he (the creator) from his mouth, arms, thighs, and feet created the Brahmin, Kshatriya and Vaishya, and the Shudra. The Brahmin, Kshatriya (and) Vaishya (constitute) the three twice-born castes, but the fourth the Shudra has only one birth. In this he was, no doubt, merely following his predecessors. But he went a step further and enunciated another proposition in which he said; Veda is the only and ultimate sanction for Dharma.

Bearing in mind that the Purusha Sukta is a part of the Veda, it cannot be difficult to realise that Manu invested the social ideal of Chaturvarna contained in the Purusha Sukta, with a degree of divinity and infallibility which it did not have before. The division of society in different classes is a universal phenomenon and India was also no exception. The number of classes has never been a matter of dogma in any society known to history. The Romans had two classes. The Egyptians had three. The Indo Iranian also had no more than three classes. The scheme of Purusha Sukta divides the society into four classes as a matter of dogma, no more no less.

4.2.3

Every society leaves a class to find its place vis-à-vis, other classes, according to its importance in society as may be determined by the forces operating from time to time. No society has official gradation laid down fixed and permanent with an ascending scale of reverence and a descending scale of contempt. The scheme of Purusha Sukta is unique in as much as it fixes a permanent warrant of precedence among the different classes, which neither time nor circumstance can alter. The warrant of precedence is based on the principle of graded inequality among the four classes, whereby it recognises the Brahmin to be above all, the Kshatriya below the Brahmin but above the Vaishya and the Shudra, the Vaishya below the Kshatriya but above the Shudra and the Shudra below all.

4.3

One of the riddles, which emerge out of sociological scrutiny of the Purusha Sukta, is the one relating to the position of the Shudra. The Purusha Sukta concerns itself with the origin of the classes and says they were created by God – a doctrine which no theology has thought it wise to propound. This is a strange thing. But what astonishes us is the plan of equating different classes to different parts of the body of the creator. The equation of the different classes to different parts of the body is not a matter of accident. It is deliberate. The idea behind this plan seems to be to discover a formula that solves two problems, one of fixing the functions of the four classes and the other of fixing the gradation of the four classes after the preconceived plan.

The Brahmin is equated to the mouth of the creator. The mouth is the noblest part of the anatomy; the Brahmin becomes the noblest of the four classes. As he is the noblest on the scale, he is given the noblest function, that of the custodian of knowledge and learning. The Kshatriya is equated to the arms of the creator. Among the limbs of a person, arms are next below the mouth. Consequently, the Kshatriya is given an order of providence next below Brahmin and is given a function that second only to knowledge, namely, fighting. The Vaishyas are equated to the thighs of the creator. In the gradation of limbs, the thighs are next below the arms. Consequently, the Vaishyas is given an order of precedence next below the Kshatriya and is assigned a function of industry and trade which in name and fame ranks or rather did rank in ancient times below that of a warrior.

The Shudra is equated to the feet of the creator. The feet form the lowest and the most ignoble part of the human frame. Accordingly, the Shudra is placed last in the social order and is given the filthiest function, namely, to serve as a menial. The later developments of Chaturvarna are mainly two; the first is the creation of the fifth class next below the Shudras. The second is the separation of the Shudras from the first three varnas by expressing with peculiar terms as Savarnas, Avarnas,

Dvijas, non-Davijas, and Traivarnikas. They stand to indicate the subdivision of the original four classes and the relative degree of a separate position of these classes. Savarna means one who belongs to any one of the four varnas.

Avarnas means one who does not belong to any one of the four varnas. The Brahmins, Kshatriya, Vaishyas, and Shudras are Savarnas. The Untouchables or Ati-Shudras are called Avarnas, those who have no Varna. Dvijay is generally contracted with non Dvijaya. Dvijay means twice-born, having the right to Upanayana and non Davija means are who is born only once. The Upanayana is treated the second birth. Those who have the right to wear the sacred thread are called Dvijay. Those who have no right to wear the sacred thread are called non-Davijas. The Brahmins, Kshatriyas, and Vaishyas have the right to wear the sacred thread, logically, they are Dvijay. The Shudras and the Ati-Shudras have no right to wear the sacred thread, logically they are both non-Davijay. The Traivarnika is contrasted with the Shudras.

4.4

The Brahminic theory of the origin and status of the Shudras

4.4.1

Here is a complete collection of all the Brahminic speculation on the origin of the four classes and the Shudras. The ancient Brahmins were conscious of the fact that the origin of the four classes was an unusual and uncommon social phenomenon and that the place of the Shudra in it was very unnatural and that this called for some explanation. Otherwise would be impossible to account for these innumerable attempts to explain the origin of the Chaturvarna and the Shudras. The variety of them is simply bewildering. Some allege that Purusha was the origin of the four varnas and some attribute their origin to Brahma, some to Prajapati, and some to Vratya. The same source gives differing explanations; the White Yajurveda has two explanations, one in terms of Purusha, the other in terms of Prajapati.

The Black Yajur Veda has three explanations to offer. Two are in terms of Prajapati, the third in terms of Brahmin. The Atharva Veda has four explanations, one in terms of Purusha, second in terms of Brahmin, third in terms of Vartya, and fourth quite different from the first three. Even when the theory is the same, the details are not the same. Some explanations such as those in terms of Prajapati, or Brahma are theological; others in terms of Manu or Kasyapa are in humanistic terms. Turning to the Brahminic view of the civil status of the Shudras, what strikes one is the long list of disabilities accompanied by the direst system of pains and penalties to which the Shudra is subjected by the Brahminic lawgivers.

4.4.2

The disabilities and penalties of the Shudras found in the Samhitas and the Brahmanas may be summarised under the following heads:

1. That the Shudras was to take the last place in the social order.

2. That the Shudras was impure and therefore no sacred act should be done within his sight and hearing.

3. That the Shudra is not to be respected in the same way as the other classes

4. That the life of a Shudra is of no value and anybody may kill him without having to pay compensation and if at all of the small value as compared with that of the Brahmin, Kshatriya, and Vaishya.

5. That the Shudra must not acquire knowledge and it is a sin and crime to educate him.

6. That a Shudra must not acquire property. A Brahmin can take his property at his pleasure

7. That a Shudra cannot hold office under the state.

8. That the duty and salvation of the Shudra lie in his serving the higher classes.

9. That the higher classes must not inter-marry with the Shudra. They can however keep a Shudra woman as a concubine. But if the Shudra touches a woman of the higher classes he will be liable to be dire consequences.

10. That the Shudra is born in servility and must be kept in servility forever.

What mischief the Dharma Sutras and the Smritis have done in imposing the disabilities upon the Shudra? The imposition of the disabilities would not have been so atrocious if the disabilities were dependent upon the condition and if the disabled had the freedom to outgrow those conditions. But what the Brahminic law does is not merely to impose disabilities but it tries to fix the conditions by making an act that amounts to a breach of those conditions to be a crime involving dire punishment. Thus the Brahminic law not only seeks to impose disabilities but it endeavours them to make permanent. The Brahminic law book merely states the disabilities. They say that the Shudras have no right to Upanayana. They say that the Shudras shall not have property. But they do not say why? The whole thing is arbitrary. The disabilities of the Shudras have no relation to his conduct. It is not the result of infamy. The Shudra is punished first because he was a Shudra.

4.5

Shudras versus Aryans

4.5.1

The Brahminic writers do not give us any clue as to who the Shudras were and how they came to be the fourth Varna. Western writers have a definite theory about the origin of the Shudras. Though all of them are not agreed upon in every aspect of the theory, there are points on which there seems to be a certain amount of unity among them. They comprise the following:

1. The people who created the Vedic literature belonged to the Aryan race

2. This Aryan race came from outside India and invaded India.

3. The natives of India were known as Dasas and Dasyus who were racially different from the Aryans.

4. The Aryans were a white race. The Dasas and Dasyus were a dark race.

5. The Aryans conquered the Dasas and Dasyus.

6. The Dasas and Dasyus after they were conquered and enslaved were called Shudras.

7. The Aryans cherished colour prejudice and therefore formed the Chaturvarna a whereby they separated the

white race from the Black race such as the Dasas and the Dasyus.

These are the principal elements in the western theory about the origin and position of the Shudras in the Indo-Aryan society. Whether it is valid or not is another matter. But this much must certainly be said about it that after reading the Brahminic theories with their long and tedious explanation attempting to treat a social fact as a divine dispensation, one cannot but feel a certain amount of relief in having before oneself a theory, which proceeds to give a natural explanation of a social fact. One can do nothing with the Brahminic theories except to call them senseless ebullitions of a silly mind. They have the problem as it is. With the modern theory, one is at least on the road to recover one's way.

4.5.2

To test the validity of the theory the best thing to do is to examine it with the support of evidence.

The foundation on which the whole fabric of the theory rests is the proposition that there lived a people who were Aryans by race.

Applying measures of anthropometry Prof. Ripley, an authority on the question of race has concluded that the European people belong to three different races in terms of cephalic and facial Index.

Is there an Aryan race in the physical sense of the term? There seem to be two views on the subject. One view is in favour of the existence of the Aryan race and the other not. According to the first view:

"The Aryan type – is marked by a relatively long head (dolichocephalism); a straight finely cut (liporahine) nose; a long symmetrically narrow face; well-developed regular features and a high facial angle. The stature is fairly high – and the general build of the figure well proportional and slender rather than massive.

The other view is that of Prof. Max Miller according to him, the word is used in three different senses. This is what he, in his lectures on the science of language says:

"In ar or Ara, I recognise one of the oldest names of the earth, as the ploughed land, lost in Sanskrit but preserved in Greek as (era) so that Arya would have conveyed originally the meaning of landholder, cultivator of the land, while Vaishya from vis meant householder, Ida the daughter of Manu is another name of the cultivated earth and probably a modification of Ara." The second sense in which it was used to convey the idea of ploughing or tilling the soil. As to this, Prof. Max Miller makes the following observation:

"I can only state that the etymological signification of Arya seems to be: one who ploughs or tills. The Aryans would seem to have chosen this name for themselves as opposed to the nomadic races, the Turanians, whose original name Tura implies the swiftness of the horseman." In the third sense, the word was used as a general name for the Vaishyas i.e. the general body of the people who formed the whole mass of the people. For this, Prof. Max Miller relies on Panini (III.1103) for his authority. Then there is the fourth sense, which the word got only towards the later period, in which sense it means of noble origin.

What is however of particular importance in the opinion of Prof. Max Muller on the question of the Aryan race. According to him, "There is no Aryan race in blood, Aryan is scientific language is utterly inapplicable to race. It means language and nothing but language, and if we speak of the Aryan race at all, we should know that it means no more than – Aryan speech."

The two views are obviously not in harmony. According to one view, the Aryan race existed in a physiological sense with typical hereditary traits with a fixed cephalic and facial index. According to Prof. Max Muller, the Aryan race existed in a philological sense as a people speaking a common language.

In this conflict of views, one may well ask. What is the testimony of Vedic literature? An examination of the Vedic literature shows that there occur two words in the Rig-Veda one is Arya with a small (a) and the other is Arya with a long (a). The word Arya with a short (a) is used in Rig-Veda in eighty-eight places. The word is used in four different senses: (i) enemy (ii) respectable person (iii) name for India and (iv) owner, Vaishya, or citizen.

The word Arya with long (a) is used in Rig-Veda in thirty-one places. But in none of these is the word used in the sense of race.

From the foregoing discussion, the one indisputable conclusion which follows is the terms 'Arya' and 'Arya' which occur in the Vedas have not been used in the racial sense at all.

One may also ask: what is the evidence of anthropometry? The Aryan race is described as long-headed. This description is not enough. There are two races, Teutonic and Mediterranean are long-headed. The question of which of two is the Aryan race, still remains open.

4.6

Invasion or not?

4.6.1

From where the Aryan race came into India? On the question of locating the original home of the Aryan race, there is a bewildering variety of views and opinions. According to Benfey, the original home of the Aryan race must be determined by reference to the common vocabulary. He discarded the theory of the original home of Aryans as the region eastward of the Caspian based on the absence from the primitive Aryan vocabulary of common names of two great Asiatic beasts of prey, the lion and the tiger or the beast of transport, the camel; is difficult to explain on the theory of the migration of the Aryans from the region eastward of the Caspian. Geiger finding himself in the same camp but according to him the home of the Aryans, more to the Northwest, in Central and Western Germany. He bases his conclusion largely on the three names which belong to the primitive Aryan vocabulary. In addition to the fir, the willow, the ash, the aider, and the hazel, he thinks the name of the birch, the beech, and the oak is especially decisive.

Another school holds that the original home of the Aryans race was in Caucasia because the Caucasians like the Aryans are blonds; have straight sharp noses, and handsome faces. But Prof. Ripley's view is different on the point because neither this type of blond occurs in the vicinity of the Caucasia or any native tribe making use of the Aryan language. Mr. Tilak's opinion regarding the original home of the Aryans race was in the Arctic region based on the astronomer and climatic phenomenon in the region around the North Pole.

Here we have two distinct sets of different or special characteristics of the polar and circumpolar regions-characteristics which are not found anywhere else on the surface of the globe.

4.6.2

Rig-Veda is the earliest book available on Indian society. There is no iota of evidence of invasion of Aryans from outside and the subjugation of the native tribes by them. A careful examination of the Mantras where the words Arya, Dasa, and Dasyus occur indicates that they refer not to race but cult. These words occur mostly in Rig-Veda Samhita where Arya occurs about thirty-three times in mantras which contain 153972 words on the whole. The rare occurrence itself is proof that the tribes that called themselves Aryas were not invaders that conquered the country and exterminated the people, for an invading tribe, would naturally boast of its achievements constantly.

So far as Vedic literature is concerned, it is against the theory that the original home of the Aryans was outside India. The language in which reference to the seven rivers is made in the Rig-Veda (X.75.5) is very significant. As Prof. D. S. Trivedi says – The rivers are addressed as my Ganges, my Yamuna, my Saraswati, and so on. No foreigner would ever address a river in such familiar and endearing terms unless by long association he had developed an emotion about it.

4.6.3

As to the question of conquest and subjugation references can undoubtedly be found in the Rig-Veda where Dasas and Dasyus are described as enemies of the Aryas.

The reference regarding wars between the Aryans on the one hand and the Dasa or Dasyus on the other is made in Rig-Veda. Out of thirty-three places in which the word Arya occurs in Rig-Veda, it is used only in eight places in opposition to Dasas and only in seven places, it is used in opposition to the word Dasyus. This may show the occurrence of sporadic wars between the two. It is certainly not evidence of conquest or subjugation.

The second point about the Dasas is whatever conflict there was between them and the Aryans, the two seem to have arrived at a mutual settlement based on peace with honour.

The third point to note is that whatever the degree of conflict, it was not a conflict of race. It was a conflict which had arisen on account of difference of religions.

The theory of Aryan invasion is an invention. The theory is based on nothing but pleasing assumption and inferences. Also, it is a perversion of scientific investigation. It is not allowed to enclave out of facts. On the contrary, the theory is preconceived and facts are selected to prove it.

4.6.4

The theory of the Aryan race is just an assumption and no more. It is based on a philological proposition put forth by Dr. Bopp in his epoch-making book called "Comparative Grammar" which appeared in 1835. In this book, Dr. Bopp demonstrated that a greater number of languages of Europe and some languages of Asia must be referred to as a common ancestral speech. The European languages and Astaic languages to which Bopp's proposition applied are called Indo-Germanic. Collectively, they have come to be called the Aryan languages largely because

Vedic language refers to the Aryas and is also of the same family as the Indo-Germanic. This assumption is the major premise on which the theory of the Aryan race is based.

This invention is necessary because of gratuitous assumption which underlines the western theory. The assumption is that the Indo-Germanic people are the purest of the modern representation of the original Aryan race. Its first home is assumed to have been somewhere in Europe. These assumptions raise a question. How could the Aryan speech have come to India? This question can be answered only by the supposition that the Aryans must have come into India from outside. Hence the necessity for inventing the theory of invasion.

The next assumption is that the Aryans were a superior race. This theory has its origin in the belief that the Aryans are a European race and as a European race it is presumed to be superior to the Asiatic races. Having assumed its superiority, the next logical step one is driven to take is to establish the fact of superiority, knowing that nothing can prove the superiority of the Aryan race better than invasion and conquest of native races, the western writers have proceeded to invent the story of the invasion of India by the Aryans and the conquest by them of the Dasas and Dasyus.

The next assumption is that the European races were white and had a colour prejudice against the dark races. The Aryans being a European race, it is assumed that it must have colour prejudice. The theory proceeds to find evidence to colour prejudice in the Aryans who came into India. This is found in the Chaturvarna- an institution by the established Indo-Aryans after they came to India and which according to the scholars is based upon Varna which is taken by them to mean colour.

The assertion that the Aryans came from outside and invaded India is not proved and the premise that the Dasas and Dasyus are aboriginal tribes of India is demonstratively false.

The originators of the Aryan race theory are so eager to establish their case that they have no patience to see what absurdities they land themselves in. They start on a mission to prove what they want to prove and do not hesitate to pick such evidence from the Vedas as they think is good for them.

Prof. Micheal Foster has somewhere said that 'hypothesis is the salt of science. Without a hypothesis, there is no possibility of fruitful investigation. But it is equally true that where the desire to prove a particular hypothesis is dominant, the hypothesis becomes the poison of science. The Aryan race theory of western scholars is as good an illustration of how hypothesis can be the poison of science as one can think of.

4.7

Why Theory Retained

Western Theory draws conclusions that Vedas neither identify any Aryan race nor any evidence of invasion in India by Aryans. Even Vedas do not support the contention of any racial or colour distinction among Aryans, Dasas, and Dasyus. The Aryan race theory is so absurd that it ought to have been dead long ago. But far from being dead, the theory received support from Brahmin scholars. Brahmin claims to be representative of the Aryan race and he regards the rest of the Hindus as descendants of non-Aryans. The theory helps him to establish his kinship with the European races and share their arrogance and superiority.

4.8

Aryans against Aryans

4.8.1

Enough has been said to how leaky is the Aryan theory expounded by western scholars and glibly accepted by their Brahmin fellows. Those who uphold the theory of an Aryan race invading India and conquering the Dasas and Dasyus fail to take note of certain verses in the Rig-Veda. These verses are of crucial importance. To build up a theory of an Aryan race marching into India from outside and conquering the non-Aryan native tribes without reference to these verses is utter futility. They are reproduced as follows:

1. Rig-Veda vi. 33.3. – "Oh Indra, Thou hast killed both of our opponents, the Dasas and the Aryas.

2. Rig-Veda vi. 60.3. – "Indra and Agni – these protectors of the good and righteous suppress the Dasas and Aryas who hurt us."

3. Rig-Veda, vii. 81.1. – Indra and Varuna killed the Dasas and Aryas who were the enemies of Sudas and thus protected Sudas from them."

4. Rig-Veda, viii. 24.27. – Oh you, Indra, who saved us from the hands of cruel Rakshasas and the Aryas living on the banks of the Indus, do thou deprive the Dasas of their weapons."

5. Rig-Veda, x. 38.3. – "Oh you much revered Indra, those Dasas and Aryas who are from the Aryas living on the banks of the banks of the Indus, do thou deprive the Dasas of their weapon."

6. Rig-Veda, x. 86.19. – "Oh You Mameyu, you give him all powers who pray you. With your help, we will destroy our Arya and our Dasyus enemies."

If the author of these verses of Rig-Veda were Aryans then the idea which these verses convey is that there were two different communities of Aryas who were not only different but oppose and inimical to each other. The existence of two Aryas is not a mere matter of conjecture or interpolation. It is a fact in support of which there is abundant evidence.

There is enough evidence scattered through the whole of Brahminic literature of the existence of the two different ideologies particularly related to the creation, which again point to the existence of the two different Aryan races. The comparison of these two ideologies (divine and human origin) set down in the following proposition:

1. One is sacerdotal in colour and character the other is secular.

2. One refers to a human being Manu as the progenitor; the other refers to God Brahma or Prajapati as the originator.

3. One is historical into a drift, the other is supernatural.

4. One aims at explaining the four varnas, the other aims at explaining the origin of the society only.

5. One speaks of the deluge; the other is completely silent about it.

These differences are many and fundamental, particularly fundamental seems to be the difference regarding Chaturvarna. All that has happened is that instead of one we have two explanations of Chaturvarna, supernatural Chaturvarna produced by Purusha, and natural Chaturvarna as developed among Manu's sons. That the result are so clumsy that the two ideologies are fundamentally are different and irreconcilable. To Ambedkar, it seems that they are the ideologies of two different Aryan races – one believing in Chaturvarna and the other not believing in Chaturvarna – who at a later stage became merged into one.

4.8.2

The third and the most unimpeachable evidence in support of the view come from the anthropometrical survey of the Indian people. Such a survey was first made by Sir Herbert Risley in 1901 based on a cephalic index; he concluded that the people of India were a mixture of four different races (i) Aryan, (ii) Dravidian (iii) Mongolian, and (iv) Scythian. His conclusions have been tested by Dr. Guha in 1936. Dr. Guha concludes that the Indian people are composed of two racial stocks (i) long-headed and short-headed and that long-headed are in the interior of India and the short-headed are on the outskirts.

Speaking in terms of the Alpine and the Mediterranean race, one can say that Indian people are composed of two stocks (i) The Mediterranean or the long-headed race and (2) the Alpine or the short-headed race.

About the Mediterranean race, certain facts are admitted. It is admitted that it is a race that spoke the Aryan language. It is admitted that its home was in Europe round about the Mediterranean basin and from thence it migrated to India. From its localisation, it is clear that it must have come to India before the entry of the Alpine race.

Similar facts about the Alpine race remain to be ascertained. The first is about the home of the Alpine race and the second is about its native speech. According to Prof. Ripley, the home of the Alpine race was in Asia somewhere in the Himalayas.

From the foregoing statement of facts, it will be seen that there is a solid foundation in anthropometry and history, in support of the Rig-Veda that there were in India two Aryan races and not one.

4.9

The number of Varnas, three or four?

4.9.1

Originally there were only three Varnas among the Indo-Aryans. The first piece of evidence is the Rig-Veda itself. Some scholars maintain that the Varna system did not exist in the age of the Rig-Veda. This statement is based on the view that the Purusha Sukta is an interpolation that has taken place long after the Rig-Veda was closed.

Even accepting that the Purusha Sukta is a later interpolation, it is not possible to accept the statement that the Varna system did not exist in the time of the Rig-Veda. Such a system is in open conflict with the text of the Rig-Veda. For, the Rig-Veda, apart from the Purusha Sukta does mention Brahmins, Kshatriyas, and Vaishyas not once but many times. The Brahmins are mentioned as a separate Varna fifteen times, Kshatriya nine times. What is important is that the Rig-Veda does not mention Shudra as a separate Varna. If Shudras were a separate Varna there is no reason why the Rig-Veda should not have mentioned them. The true conclusion to be drawn from the Rig-Veda is not that the

Varna system did not exist, but there were only three varnas and that Shudras were not regarded as a fourth and a separate Varna.

4.9.2

The second piece of evidence is the testimony of the two Brahmanas, the Satpatha and the Tattiriya. Both speak of the creation of three varnas only. They do not speak of the creation of the Shudra as a separate.

The Satpatha Brahmana Says:

II.1.4.11 – "Uttering, 'Bhuh' Prajapati generated this earth. (Uttering) 'Bhuvah' he generated the air, and (uttering) 'svah' he generated the sky. This universe is co-extensive with these worlds. (The fire) is placed with the whole, saying 'bhuh' Prajapati generated the Brahmin, saying 'bhuvah' he generated the Kshatriya, (and saying) svah; he generated the 'Vis'. The fire is placed with the whole (saying) bhuh', Prajapati generated offspring; he generated animals. This world is so much as self, offspring; and animals. (The fire) is placed with the whole.

The Tattiriya Brahmana says:

III.12.9.2. – This entire (universe) has been created by the Brahma. Men say that the Vaishya class was produced from ric verses. They say that the Yajur Veda is the womb from which the Kshatriya was born. The Sama Veda is the source from which the Brahmin sprang.

An inference from the Rig-Veda and two statements from two Brahmanas, which in point of authority is co-equal with the Vedas, for both are Shruti, both say indefinite and precise terms that there were only three Varnas. Both agree that the

Shudras did not form a separate and a distinct Varna, much less the fourth Varna. There cannot, therefore, be better evidence in support of the contention that there were originally only three varnas and that the Shudras were only a part of the second varna.

4.10

Brahmins Versus Shudras

4.10.1

Originally it was a three varna system in Rig–Vedic society which subsequently turned into Chaturvarna as a result of the degradation of Shudras from the second varna to the fourth varna. The degradation of the Shudras from the second varna to the fourth varna is the result of violent conflict between Brahmins and Shudras whose direct evidence is found in Vedic literature. The conflict can better be understood if the relationship between Vashishtha and Vishwakarma is traced.

The enmity between these two is a known fact to all and abundant evidence on it is found in literature such as in Harivamsa, Vishnu Purana, Markandaya Purana, and Adi Purana of Mahabharta, etc. There are particular instances in which Vashishtha and Vishvamitra had come into a conflict of general enmity with each other. This enmity was so much so that Vishvamitra wanted even to murder Vashishtha as described in Satyaparvan of Mahabharta. This enmity was not just the enmity between the two priests but between Brahmin Priest and Kshatriya Priest, Vashishtha being Brahmin and Vishvamitra being Kshatriya and of a royal lineage. The basis of the enmity between them was not personal but for the superiority, rights, and privileges of their respective varnas to which they belong, especially on the right to receive gifts, the right to teach Vedas, and the right to officiate sacrifice were the Brahmins claimed their exclusive privileges which the Kshatriyas denied the exclusiveness.

The story of Trishanku narrated in Ramayana confirms the dispute between these two particularly on the point of the right to officiate sacrifice. In this dispute between Vashishtha and Vishvamitra, Sudas seems to have played an important part. Vashishtha, the family Purohit of Sudas, performed his coronation ceremony and also helped him to win the battle of ten kings. Despite this, Sudas removed Vashishtha from the office of Purohit and appointed Vishvamitra in his place. This created enmity between Sudas and Vashishtha. There was another deed that Sudas committed which widened and intensified the enmity. Sudas threw the son of Vashishtha, Shakti into the fire and burnt him alive. It is described in Satyana Brahmana. It is also reported in the commentary on Katyayanas Anuhrammnika to the Rig-Veda. This enmity between Sudas and Vashishtha further spread to their sons which were reported in Tattiriya Samhita. This is not the only conflict between the kings and Brahmins.

4.10.2

One other conflict between king Vena and the Brahmin is reported in Hansvamsha. The next king who came in conflict with the Brahmins was Pururavas, the son of Ila and grandson of Manu Vaivasvat. The details of the conflict are told in Adi Parvan of Mahabharta.

The other king in the series is Nahusa, the grandson of Pururavas. The story of this conflict is told in two places in Mahabharata, once in the Vanaparvan and again in the Udoyaparvan. Another king in conflict with the Brahmins was Nimi whose story is told in Vishnu Purana.

The conflict between the Kings and Brahmins was the conflict between Shudras and Brahmins but unfortunately, this fact was not prominently reported. Sudas was a Shudra king. The others have not been described as Shudras but as the descendants of Ikshvaka. Sudas is also described as a descendant of Ikshvaka, so all these kings are Shudras. Manu has described these conflicts between Brahmin and Kshatriyas as he had no idea about them. In a sense, the conflict was indeed between the Brahmins and Kshatriyas because the Shudras were also a branch of Kshatriyas. It would however have been far more illuminating if they had been described in more precise terms as conflicts between Brahmins and Shudras. Understood as a history of conflict between Brahmins and Shudras, it helps one to understand how the Shudras came to be degraded from the second to the fourth Varna.

4.11

The Degradation of the Shudras

4.11.1

Now it is explicit that Shudras were degraded to the fourth varna from the second varna as vengeance upon the Shudras by the Brahmins because of violent conflict between the Brahmins and Shudras. In the opinion of Ambedkar, the technique the Brahmins used to degrade the Shudras was the denial to perform the Upanayana for the Shudras. The Upanayana ceremony had great importance in Indo-Aryan society. The purpose of

Upanayana was to initiate a person in the study of Vedas which commenced with the teaching of Gayatri Mantra and wearing of sacred thread called Yajnopavita. Later on, the Upanayana has come to be the wearing of the sacred thread, Yajnopavita.

The ceremony of Upanayana was not an empty ceremony. It bears with it the right to have the knowledge and the right to have property. The rules are laid down in Purva Mimansha. Firstly, the property is meant primarily for a person with the means of performing a sacrifice. The right to property is dependent upon the capacity to sacrifice and in turn, capacity to sacrifice depends upon Upanayana. Secondly, the sacrifice must be accompanied by Veda mantras. This means that the sacrifice must have undergone a course in Vedas. A person who has not studied vedas is not competent to perform the sacrifice.

The study of Veda is open to only those persons who have undergone the Upanayana ceremony. In other words, who has not performed the ceremony of Upanayana, the right to have the knowledge and the right to have property are closed for him. Once the relation to education and property is grasped, all difficulty in accepting the thesis that the degradation of the Shudras was entirely due to the loss of Upanayana must vanish.

4.11.2

Is the absence of Upanayana the test of Shudradom?

In order to find out what the courts in India have regarded as the surest criterion determining who is a Shudra, some judicial decisions may be referred to. The first case to which reference may be made is to be found in 7, M.I.A. 18. It was decided by the Privy Council in 1837. The question at issue was whether at the relevant time there was in India any Kshatriya. The contention of one side was that there were and on the other side, there were none. The latter contention was based upon the theory propagated by the Brahmins that the Brahmin Parsurama had killed all the Kshatriyas and that if any were left they were all exterminated by the Shudra king Mahapadma Nanda, so that thereafter there were no Kshatriya left and that there were only Brahmins and Shudra. The Privy Council did not accept this theory which they regarded as false and concocted by the Brahmin and hold that the Kshatriya still existed in India.

The second case on the subject is to found in I. L. R. 10 Cal. 688. The question raised in the case was whether the Kayasthas of Bihar were Kshatriyas or Shudras. The high court decided that they were Shudras. The partisans of the Kayasthas took the position that the Kayasthas of Bihar were different from the Kayasthas of Bengal, the Upper Provinces, and Banaras and that while those in the Upper Provinces and Banaras were Shudras, the Kayasthas of Bihar were Kshatriyas. The court refused to make this distinction and held that the Kayasthas of Bihar were also Shudras. The validity of this judgement was not accepted by the Allahabad high court in I. L. R. 12 All. 328.

The third case is reported in (1916) 20 Cal. W. N. 901. Here the question raised was whether Kayasthas of Bengal were Kshatriyas or Shudra. The High court of Calcutta held that they were Shudras. The case was taken to the Privy Council by way of appeal against the decision of the Calcutta High Court. The decision of the Privy Council is reported in (1926) 47 I.A. 140. The question of whether the Bengali Kayasthas are Shudras or Kshatriyas was not decided upon by the Privy Council but was left open. In between 1916 and 1926 the Calcutta High Court gave two decisions which held that the intermarriages between Kayasthas of Bengal and Tantis and Domes (the two of the low castes), were legal on the ground that both of them were subcastes of Shudras.

These decisions which caused further deterioration in the position of the Kayasthas were followed by another which is reported in I. L. R. 6 Patna 506. In a most elaborate judgement extending over forty-seven pages, Mr. Justice Jwala Prasad went into every Purana and every Smriti in which there was a reference to the Kayasthas. He differed from the Calcutta high court and held that the Kayanthas of Bihar were Kshatriyas.

4.11.3

Next comes, cases in which the question at issue was whether the Marathas are Kshatriyas or Shudras. The first case in which this issue was raised is reported in 48 Mad. I. This was an interpleader suit filed by the receiver of the estate of Raja of Tanjore in which all the descendants, as well as the distant agnates and cognates of the Raja, were made defendants in the suit. The kingdom of Tanjore was founded by Venkoji, otherwise called Ekoji, who was a Maratha and the brother of Shivaji, the founder of the Maratha Empire. The judgement in the case covers 229 pages and the question of whether the Marathas were Kshatriya was dealt with in a most exhaustive manner. The Madras high court decided that the Marathas were Shudras and not Kshatriyas as was contented by the defendants.

The next case which also relates to the Marathas is repeated in I. L. R. (1928) 52 Bom. 497. The court decided that:

There are three classes among the Marathas in the Bombay Presidency: (i) the five families; (ii) the ninety-six families; (iii) the rest of these, the first two classes are Kshatriyas.

In another case in which reference may be made is reported in I. L. R. (1927) 52 Mad I. The issue was whether the Yadvas of Madura were Kshatriya. The Yadavas claimed themselves to be Kshatriyas. But the Madras high court negatived the claim and held that they were Shudras.

Such is the course of judicial pronouncements on the issue as to how to determine who is a Kshatriya and who is a Shudra. More important for our purpose are the criteria which the courts have adopted in coming to their decisions. Courts have laid down a number of criteria for different cases but the wearing of the sacred thread (Upanayan) is sound according to Ambedkar for judging the status of a person whether he is Kshatriya or Shudra among others.

4.11.4

Did the Shudras ever have the right to Upanayana?

Primitive society does not begin with differentiation. It begins with uniformity and ends in diversity. The natural thing would be to suppose that in the matter of the Upanayana the ancient Aryan society treated all its classes on the same footing. The ancient Aryan society regarded Upanayana as essential for all.

The six anuloma castes were also eligible for Upanayana; this is clear from the rules for the Upanayana of Kshatriya, Vaishyas, and mixed castes like Rathakara, Ambastha, etc. The proper age for the Upanayana of a Brahmin was the 8th year from birth, of a Kshatriya 11th year, and a Vaishay 12th year. As to the Shudras, the evidence is equally positive. If Sudas was a king, if Sudas was a Shudra, if his coronation ceremony was performed by Vashishtha and he performed the Rajasuya Yaga, then there can be no doubt that the Shudras had at one time won the sacred thread. In addition to circumstantial evidence and the evidence of the authors mentioned before the Sanskara Ganapati cited by Max Muller contains an express provision declaring the Shudra to be eligible for Upanayana.

4.11.5

When Upanayana was open to everyone, Aryan or non-Aryan, it was not a matter of social significance. It was a common right of all. It was not a privilege of the few. Once it was denied to the Shudras, its possession became a matter of honour and its denial a badge of servility. The denial of Upanayana to the Shudras introduced a new factor in the Indo Aryan society. It made the Shudras look up to the higher classes as their superior and enabled the three higher classes to look down upon the Shudras as their inferiors. This is one way in which the loss of Upanayana brought about the degradation of the Shudras.

It will be seen from what has been said above, how the sacrament of Upanayana was in the ancient Aryan society fundamental and how the social stakes and personal rights of persons depended upon it. Without Upanayana, a person was doomed to social degradation, ignorance, and poverty. The stoppage of Upanayana was a most deadly weapon discovered by the Brahmins to avenge themselves against the Shudra. It had the effect of an atomic bomb. It did make the Shudra, to use the language of the Brahmins, a graveyard.

That the Brahmins possessed the power to deny Upanayana is beyond question. An account is taken of two things

1. The exclusive right of the Brahmin to officiate at the Upanayana.

2. The penalties imposed upon the Brahmin for performing unauthorised Upanayana.

One thing therefore must be taken as well established, namely that none but a Brahmin could perform the Upanayana ceremony, Upanayana performed by anybody else is not a valid Upanayana. The other operative part of the Indo-Aryan religious system is the obligation imposed upon the Brahmin not to do any unauthorised act of a religious character. A Brahmin guilty of any such conduct was liable to punishment or penance. The combined effect of these two factors was to vest in the Brahmin the power of performing as well as of denying Upanayana.

4.11.6

The coronation ceremony of Shivaji, itself, is direct evidence of it.

Shivaji established a Hindu independent kingdom in Western Maharashtra. For proclaiming as a king himself a coronation ceremony by Brahmin according to Vedic rites needs to be performed. But for the performance of the coronation ceremony, one has to prove himself as Kshatriya and had performed the Upanayana at the relevant age which is the eleventh year in the case of Kshatriyas. As regards the difficulty of Upanayana could be got over by the performance of the Vratya stoma ceremony. The greatest stumbling block was Shivaji's status. Shivaji's claim that he was Kshatriya was opposed by many Brahmins including his own Prime Minister Moro Pant Pingle. In their view, he was Shudra and that he was not entitled to have coronation performed as it was a right that belonged to the Kshatriya only.

Shivaji was, however, succeeded in securing the services of one Gagabhat, a renowned Brahmin, resident of Benaras, learned in vedas and shastras. Gagabhat solved all difficulties and performed Shivaji's coronation on 6th June 1674 at Riagad, first after performing the Vratya stoma and then the Upanayana. Shivaji's case is important because it proves that nobody except a Brahmin has the right to perform the Upanayana and that nobody can compel him to perform if he is not prepared to do so. Also, it is important because it proves that the power of determining the status of a Hindu depends entirely upon the will of the Brahmins. The decision in favour of Shivaji is sought to be justified by the geneology which was brought from Mewar by Shivaji's friend Balaji Avaji, and which connected Shivaji with the Sisodiyas of Mewar who were reckoned as Kshatriyas. It has been alleged that the geneology was a fabrication got up for the occasion.

Assuming it was not a fabrication, how can it justify the recognition of Shivaji's claim to be a Kshatriya? Far from establishing that Shivaji was Kshatriya, the geneology could do no more than raising another question, namely, whether the Sisodiyas were Kshatriyas. The Sisodiyas were Rajputs. There is considerable doubt as to whether the Rajputs are the descendants of the original Kshatriyas who formed the second varna of the ancient Indo-Aryan community. One view is that they are foreigners, remnants of the Huns who invaded

India and established themselves in Rajputana and whom the Brahmins raised to the status of Kshatriya with the object of using them as means to suppress Buddhism in central India, by a social ceremony before the sacred fire and who were therefore known as the Agnikul Kshatriyas. This view has the support of many erudite scholars who are entitled to speak on the subject.

The case of Shivaji is also important because the decisions of the Brahmins on the matter of status were open to sale. That the decision of the Gagabhat was not an honest decision is obvious from the amount of money that Gagabhat and other Brahmins received as officiating priests. Gagabhat gave his opinion that Shivaji was Kshatriya and that he was prepared to perform his coronation and even went so far as to write a treatise known as Gagabhatti.

Shivaji was recognised as a Kshatriya. Obviously, that status was not a personal honour conferred on him. It was a status in the tail and belonged to his family as well as descendants. Nobody could question it. It could be lost by a particular descendant by doing some act that was inconsistent with it. It could not be lost generally. No act inconsistent with the Kshatriya status was attributed to any of the descendants of Shiva Ji, yet the Brahmins came forward to repudiate the decisions on their status.

This could happen only because the Brahmins claimed the power to do and undo the status of any Hindu at any time. They can raise a Shudra to the status of Kshatriya. They can degrade the Kshatriya to the status of a Shudra. Shivaji's case proves that their sovereignty in this matter is without limit and challenge.

4.12

History of Word Dalit

4.12.1

In the Rig-Veda, we find often mention of slaves, sometimes in large numbers, and wealth was to some extent made up of ownership of slaves. As the word Dasa became in the later literature synonymous with slave, we may suppose that the slaves were taken almost entirely from among the conquered non-Aryans. The Purusha Sukta which describes practically the creation of the universe and inhabitants does not mention the Dasa but gives the name of Shudra instead. The word Shudra does not occur anywhere else in the Rig-Veda. In the later period, Shudra denoted a slave.

4.12.2

Mahatma Gandhi described the untouchables 'Harijans 'signifying 'the Children of God'. In a very short period, the word became popular and was used in general parlance for calling untouchables 'Harijan.' The earliest reference of the word is found in Tulsidas's Ramayana wherein Lakshman describes the characteristic of Kshatriya that a Kshatriya must not use force against a god, a Brahmin, a Harijan, and a cow. The word Harijan is also found in the "Bhajan Vaishnava Jana To" by Nar Singh Mehta, a Vaishnavite poet from Gujrat. Ambedkar vehemently rejected calling Harijan by Gandhi to the oppressed and despised classes rather he called them untouchables which was the actual physically social position of the classes and in his opinion, Gandhi was running away from realising the actual position under the guise of word Harijan. In 1877 the Bombay

Gazette described this class of people by the term 'Depressed Classes'. From 1916 the British Government used this term in official communication. Later this class was renamed as 'Scheduled Castes, in 1935 by the Govt. of India Act which still continues in the official parlance.

4.12.3

Etymologically the origins of the term Dalit can be traced to the Buddhas usage of the Pali dallida in the Dallida Sutta, said to have been preached at the Kalenda Karnivapa in Rajegah (Samyutte Nihaya XI.14) in Pali Buddhist literature, the term Dalidda (*daridra* in Sanskrit) is used to the property less poor in contrast to the gahapati class of the rich. Nalin Swaris (2011, 99) citing Angullara Nikaya (III.84) says" the Dalida hulls, the pauper lineage, is described as people without enough to eat and drink, without even a covering for their back. The Dalit leader, A.N.Rajbhog founded the Journal Dalit Bandhu (Friends of Dalit) in Pune in 1928.

The term has been used in western India in this sense at least since Jyotiba Phule's (1827-90) time. Phule is supposed to have used Dalit in terms of Dalituthan (upliftment of the downtrodden) but the evidence is anecdotal (Louis 2003-144). Phule used the term Ati-Shudras for untouchables in his writings. The founding of the militant organisation Dalit Panthers in 1972 in Bombay gave an all- India currency to Dalit (broken, crushed people) and used it to refer not just to the untouchable communities, but to the working people, the landless and poor peasants, women and all those who are being exploited politically and economically and in the name of religion. This was a phenomenal and politically confident act of solidarity on their part. They saw Dalit as a Nation of the oppressed.

4.13

Who are scheduled tribes?

Adivasi is the collective term for the tribes of India who are considered to be indigenous people. Adivasi comprising Adi means beginning, origin, and Vasin, the dwellers, thus Adivasi signifies original inhabitants of India who are called aborigines and vanvasi also. According to Prof. Nihar Ranjan Roy central Indian adivasis are the original autochthonous people of India. The anthropologist Dr. Vernier Elwin stated this more emphatically when he writes." These are the real swadeshi product of India, in whose presence all others are foreign. They were here first and should come first[2]. By the India Government Act 1935, they were described as Scheduled Tribes acquiring the official nomenclature which is still prevalent.

Article 366 (25) of the Constitution of India defines Schedules Tribes as "such tribes or tribal communities or parts of or groups within such tribes or tribal communities as are deemed under Article 342 to be Schedules Tribes for the purpose of this Constitution. They comprise a substantial minority population of India making up 8.6% of India's population over 104 million people according to census 2011 and 86% of which is concentrated in the central belt covering the state of Madhya Pradesh, Odisha, Chhatisgarh, Jharkhand, Gujrat, Maharasthra, Rajasthan, Andhra Pradesh, and West Bengal. About 10% of their population resides in the North-Eastern states of Assam,

---

2   Guruswami Mohan, Scroll.in/article/773759/Adivasis-india-original-inhabitantants-have-suffered-themost-at-its-hands accessed on 25.04.2021

Arunachal Pradesh, Manipur, Meghalaya Mizoram, Nagaland, Tripura, and Sikkim and the remaining 4 % in the seven states of Uttar Pradesh, Uttarakhand, Himachal Pradesh, Goa, Bihar, Karnataka, Tamilnadu and six union territories of Jammu and Kashmir, Laddhak, Dadra and Nagar Haveli, Daman and Div, Lakshadweep and Andaman and Nicobar Islands (Census 2011, Jaiswal 2012169, Jaiswal 2019).

Still, predominantly the aborigines have remained in their primitive uncivilised state in a land that boasts of civilisation thousands of years old. Not only are they not civilised but some of them follow pursuits that have led to their being classified as criminals. These people living in the midst of civilisation are still in a savage state and are leading the life of hereditary criminals. Why has no attempt been made to civilise these aborigines and to lead them to take to an honourable way of making a living? Civilising the aborigines means adapting them as your own, living in their midst, and culturing fellow feeling, in short, loving them. How is it possible for a Hindu to do this? His whole life has anxious effort to preserve his caste. Caste is his precious possession which he must save at any caste. He cannot consent to lose it by establishing contact with the aborigines, the remnants of the hateful anaryas of the Vedic days.

4.14

History of Scheduled Tribes

4.14.1.

Ancient India (1500 BCE–500 CE)

Although considered uncivilised and primitive, Adivasis were usually not held to be intrinsically impure by surrounding (usually Dravidian or Aryan) caste Hindu populations, unlike Dalits who were. Thus the Adivasi origin of Valmiki who composed the Ramayana was acknowledged, as were the origins of Adivasi Tribes such as Garasia and Bilala. Unlike the subjugation of Dalits, the Adivasis often enjoyed autonomy and depending upon region, evolved mixed hunter-gatherers and forming economies, controlling their lands as a joint patrimony of the Tribe. The Meena and Ghond Rajas of Garha Mandala and Chanda are examples of an Adivasi aristocracy that ruled in the region and were not alone the hereditary leaders of their Gond subjects, but also held sway over substantial communities of non-tribal who recognised them as their feudal lords.

4.14.2

Medieval period (500 CE–1700 CE)

The relative autonomy and collective ownership of Adivasi land by Adivasis were severely disturbed by the advent of Mughals and it was the forests and mountains that offered sanctuary to the beleaguered Hindus. K.S. Lal in his book "The legacy of Muslims Rule in India" reports that there was a large surge of forests population during the Muslim rule. With the advent of the Kachwaha Rajputs and Mughals into their territory, the Meenas were gradually sidelined and pushed deep into the forests. The defeated Rajas and helpless agriculturists all sought refuge in the forests. Those who took to the Jungle, stayed there, eating with wild fruits, tree roots, and the coursed grains if and when available, but surely preserving their freedom. But with the passing of time, a peasant became a tribal and from a tribal, a beast.

And the peasant finding continuance of cultivation uneconomic and the treatment of the regime unbearable left the fields and fled into the jungle from where they organised resistances. The avalanche of Turco-Mughal invaders and the policy of their Government turned many settled agriculturists into tribals of the jungles. Many defeated Rajas and harassed Zamidars also repaired to forests and remote fortresses security.

During the medieval period and in the years and centuries of oppression, they lived almost like wild beasts in the improvised huts in villages, segregated and isolated, suffering and struggling. But by setting in forest villages, they were enabled to preserve in their Akharas, which are even now practised in different forms in many states. Such a phenomenon was not witnessed in West Asian countries. There in the vast open deserts, the people could not save themselves from forced conversions against advancing Muslim armies. There were no forests into which they could fled, hide and organise resistance. Hence they all became Muslim.

4.14.3

British Period (1700 CE–1947 CE)

From the early days of British rule, the tribal men resented the British encroachments upon their tribal system. According to K. S. Lal, "their spirit of resistance had made them good together. Fighting kept their health replenished, compensating for the non-availability of good food in jungles. The British census official labelled them, in the successive census as Aboriginals (1881), Animists (1891-1911), and as Adherents of Tribal Religions (1921-31).

Britishers faced continuous revolts from local revolts to warlike campaigns spread over larger parts. There were about 110 sporadic rebellions and seventy major revolts during the 200 years of British Rule in India. Revolts by Mal Pahariya in 1772, in Rampa areas in 1813, by Bhills in 1818-1831, by Hols of Singhbhum in 1831, by Hols in 1831-32, by Khonds in 1846, by Santhals in 1855-57, by Birsa Munda during 1874-1901 are a few important to name. Several Adivasis participated in the Indian independence movement also, including Dharindhar, Bhyuan, Laxman Naik, Jantya Bhil, Bhangaru Devi, and Rehma Vasave. What the Muslim Rule could not achieve completely, the British did by their devours policy of divide and destroy the Hindu society.

In order to neutralise them, the British developed the templates of delegitimising the resisting Hindu communities by branding them as Thugs, Criminal Tribes, etc. The Thuggees Act was passed in 1836 which was further amplified by ten enactments passed between 1836 to 1848. Mere resistance to the British was enough to brand to register as a thug and banish his entire community.

Post-1857 revolt, the British developed the second colonial template of 'give a bad name, a dog' and hang him to delegitimise and destroy the many untenable Hindus communities. Thus came the Criminal Tribes Act (CTA) in 1871, and numerous rebellious castes were labelled as Criminal Tribes under CTA, resulting whole community was presumed guilty by birth.

Pertinently, while the targeted communities were Hindu castes, the British maliciously labelled among many of them as tribes. This mischief to segregate them from the Hindu society became evident from the religion-neutral synthetic ascriptions to them in the successive census, thereby, naming them for civilising missions.

The third colonial template was the policy of segregation of Vanvasis that was attempted in the east while Madras presidency after the first Ramapa rebellion in 1813. Act XXIV of 1839 was promulgated excluding the forested areas described as Agency Tracts of Ganjan (now in Odisha) and Visakhapatnam (now in Andhra Pradesh (AP)) districts from the general administration. Its success led to the promulgation of a harsher Scheduled Districts Act 1874 in the whole of India not only excluding the Vanvasi areas from the period of general administration but from the general society as well. The Government of India Act 1935, a precursor of the Constitution of India further formalised the exclusive of Vanvasi areas by classifying them as excluded areas and partially excluded areas. As a result, general Indians became almost foreigners to these areas in their own country as they were forbidden from entering and acquiring property there.

The fourth colonial template was isolating Vanvasi from the general Hindu society by preventing physical, social, and economic contact between them. Through the Forest Act of 1865, 1878, and 1927 the British declared their monopoly over forests by truncating the millennia-old traditional use of forests by communities. For systematic exploitation, forests were declared as reserved and protected. All rights of the people over forest land and produce were extinguished. Forest offences were created whereby even entering inside the reserved or protected forest was made punishable.

4.14.5

Post Independence

Post-independence, these barriers are further amplified with a special provision as in the Fifth Schedule of the constitution. The analogous Scheduled Areas Land Transfer Regulation enacted there under by various states perpetuate with greater vigour and rigour the isolationist and destructive policies of the British. As a result, the millennia-old social, economic and religious intercourse between the Scheduled Tribes in Scheduled Areas and the people outside became scarce leading to their tribalisation and backwardness.

The Forest Rights Act 2006 though is laudable in its intent but it only furthers the same isolationist policy. The title of the land given to the Scheduled Tribes is only heritable, but not alienable or transferrable under Section 4 of the Act. By giving forest land which is not transferrable or monetisable, the Scheduled Tribes are perpetually shackled to the forest for generations. Giving land in the non-forest and non-scheduled areas would have helped the Scheduled Tribes to grow much better and join the mainstream. Alternatively suitable compact forests and scheduled areas could have been de-reserved and de-scheduled for allotments to Scheduled Tribes by developing them as new growth centres, but that was not to be.

Any development presupposes mainstreaming. An isolated community, society, or nation can never develop. Therefore removing the constitutional and legal barriers is a prerequisite to mainstream and usher in the all-around development of Scheduled Tribes in scheduled areas.

4.15

Hinduism – Adivasi roots of Modern Hinduism

4.15.1

Some historians and anthropologists assert that much of what constitutes Folk Hinduism today is actually descended from an amalgamation of Adivasi faiths, ideal worship practices, and deities. This also includes the sacred status of certain animals such as monkeys and cows and plants such as Pipal and Tulsi which may once have held totemic importance of certain Adivasi Tribes.

As the Hindu ideals are saints, sages, Avatar and so are those of the Adivasis. There is a long list of saints of prominent one is given below:

Saints

1. Sant Baddhu Bhagat led the Kol insurrection (1831-32) aimed against the tax imposed on Mundas by Muslim Rulers.

2. Sant Dhira or Kannappa Nayanar of one of sixty-three Nayanar Shaivite saints, a hunter from whom Lord Shiva gladly accepted food offerings.

3. Sant Gang Narayan led the Bhumi revolt (1832-33) aimed against Christian missionaries and British colonialists.

4. Sant Gurudev Kalicharan Brahma or Guru Brahma, a Bado who founded the Brahma Dharma aimed against Christian missionaries and colonialists. The Brahma Dharma movement sought to unite peoples of all religions to worship God together and survive even today.

5. Sant Jatra oraon led the Tana Bhagat movement (1914-19) aimed against the Christian missionaries and British colonialists.

6. Sant Tantya Mama (Bhil) a Bhil after whom a movement is named the Jananayda Tantya Bhil.

7. Sant Kalean Guru (Kalean Murmu) is the most belonged person among Santhal tribes community who was widely popular 'Nogam Guru'. Guru of Early Histories in the fourteenth century by the references of their forefathers.

Sages

Bhakta Sabari, a Nishada woman who offered Shri Ram and Shri Laxman her half-eaten ber-fruits which they gratefully accepted when they were searching for Sita in the forest.

Maharashi – Maharashi Matanga, Matanga Bhil, Guru of Bhakta Shabari. In fact Chandals are often addressed as Matanga in passages like Varaha Purana 1.139.91

Avatars

1. Birsa Bhagwan or Birsa Munda – considered an avatar of Khastra Kora. People approached him as Singbonga, the Sun god. His sect included Christian converts. He and his clan, the Mundas were connected with Vaishnavite traditions as they were influenced by Sri Chaitanya. Birsa was very close to the Parre brothers Vaishnavites.

2. Kirata – the form Lord Shiva as a hunter. It is mentioned in Mahabharta. The Karppillikkavu Sree Mahadev temple, Kerala adores Lord Shiva in this Avatar and is known to be one of the oldest surviving temples in Bharat.

3. Vettakhorumahan, the son of Lords Kirata.

4. Kalatadataka or Vaikunthanatha, Koller (robber) avtar of Lord Vishnu.

4.15.2

Other Tribal and Hinduism

Some Hindus believe that Indian tribals are close to the romantic ideal of the ancient silvan culture of the Vedic people. Mahadev Sadashiv Golwalkar said:

The tribals can be given Yajnopavita. They should be given equal rights and footing in the matter of religious rights, in temple worship, in the study of Vedas, as in general, in all our social and religious affairs. This is the only right solution for all the problems of casteism found nowadays in our Hindu society.

At the Lingaraj Temple in Bhubaneshwar, Brahmins and Badis (tribal) are priests. The Badis have the most intimate contact with the deity of the temple, and only they can bathe and adorn it. The Bhils are mentioned in Mahabharat. The Bhil boy Eqalavya's teacher was Dronacharya and he had the honour to be invited to Yudhishtras Rajasuya Yajna at Inderprastha. Indian tribals were also part of royal armies in the Ramayana and the Arthashatra.

4.16

Naxalism and Tribes in India

4.16.1

Naxalism owes its name and origin to a small incident in Naxalbari village in the state of West Bengal, in which a small group of local tribal and other backward caste cultivators rose against the feudal practices of exploitation, oppression, and atrocities involving denial of their share in agriculture produce and the payment of fair wages by upper-caste landlords. On 25th May 1967 the police opened fire on protesting persons led by three men Charu Mazumdar, Jungle Santhal, and Kanu Sanyal. Soon after this protest assumed the shape of a left-wing people's movement under the leadership of aforesaid mentioned. They demanded socio-economic justice and the eradication of an oppressive feudal system.

The movement has its ups and downs but it reached its climax in 1980 and spread beyond Bengal in other states. The Peoples War Group (PWG) was formed by Kondapalli Seetharamaiah an associate of Charu Mazumdar. PWG emerged as the most formidable Nexalite formation not only in Andhra Pradesh but also in adjoining states. Over 90% of the rural poor below the poverty line live in the twelve major states of Andhra Pradesh, Bihar, Karnataka, Madhya Pradesh, Chhatisgarh, Jharkhand, Maharashtra, Odisha, Rajasthan, Tamilnadu, Uttar Pradesh, and West Bengal. It is not a coincidence that the Naxalites are active in varying degrees in these states. The Naxalite's pro-poor ideology has strong gravitation for the youth among the student community. (Lord 2015: 86, Bhagabati 2001:7)

4.16.2

In India, about 80 million tribal are still considered to be the most vulnerable and poorest of the poor. A large section of the tribal population living below the poverty line is a victim of hunger and malnutrition. The Naxalite movement is active in the tribal areas. The root cause of Naxalites among the tribal are directly linked to social, economic, and political grievances which include, deprivation, degradation, exploitation, poverty, unemployment, illiteracy, oppression. Despite the constitutional safeguards with twin objectives of empowerment and development of tribal for their integration into the mainstream of the nation, they have been denied social, economic, and political justice and human rights.

More than 50% of them are illiterate and live below the poverty line under inhuman conditions. They are arbitrarily deprived of their land rights and rights pertaining to forests areas. Tribal are helpless victims of bad governance and exploitation, and the dwindling resource base of the tribal people can be quantified in the shape of loss of land, restriction of access to forest produce, and a lack of opportunities for reasonable wage employment.

It was in the background of utter grievance frustration of the tribal arising out of their exploitation and oppression which led to them of their taking arms in several areas of the fight for their rights under the patronage of Naxalites. In fact, over the years, the tribal insurgency has become the predominant strand of the Naxalites and people war group movement. The combination of socio-economic and political factors has led to a resurgence of left-wing extremism and Naxalite movements in India. The Naxalite ideology seeks to cut across the barriers of caste, religion and region and units people on broader economic issues.

CHAPTER FIVE

DISCRIMINATION – A GLOBAL PHENOMENON

5.1

Discrimination based on work and descent, the terminology of the United Nations for systematic discrimination like caste-based hierarchy system, is a long-standing practice for thousands of years in many societies of the world and affects a population of over 300 million. The nomenclature of this discriminatory and despised class has always been a matter of controversy, yet the discrimination determined on the basis of birth and occupation, a universal and global phenomenon, results in serious violations across the full spectrum of civil, cultural, economic, political and social rights. The discriminatory, cruel inhuman, and degrading treatment is affected by both edges of the sword for the performance of least desirable jobs in society, first from the nature of the work they perform and suffering again by the denial of their rights because they perform unacceptable work.

In Africa, such forms of discrimination exist and are practised against certain communities and passed on to generations. Such discriminatory practices against these communities often manifest whereby a considerable population is forced of the sex trade, forced labour, child slave trade, witchcraft or witch children or women, cultural, traditional, and ritual slavery. In South America, discriminatory practices exist in the form of slavery, exclusion in excess to mainstream society. In European countries, discrimination practice exists in the form of 'antiziganism or anti-gypsyism.' In South Asia, it is identified as caste-based discrimination. The affected population is referred to as Dalits. They are often harassed, beaten to death, and face exclusion in socio-economic development.

5.2

Caste system in Asia

Dalits constitute the largest caste-affected groups in South Asia. They compose a myriad of subcaste groups and, although subjected to similar forms of discrimination across the region, the situation of Dalits in caste-affected countries differs for historical and political reasons. Dalits represent the victims of the gravest form of discrimination, are often assigned the most degrading job, and subjected to forced and bonded labour, have limited or unequal access to resources (including economic resources, land, and water), and services and disproportionately affected by poverty.

5.2.1

In Sri Lanka, there are two caste systems, one for the Sinhalese and the other for the Tamils. Although they both have their origin in India, the Sinhalese caste system is not linked to the Hindu Varna. It was an aspect of a feudal society that divided people "according to Descent and Blood" or according to their hereditary roles and functions. The caste system was a secular hierarchy. The exception is the caste of Rodiyas or Rodi (meaning *filth*) from very early times.

Many legends surround their origin, all agreeing that they were banished for a heinous crime and condemned to a life of begging or, more accurately, soliciting for alms. They were denied land and work and subjected to many disadvantages and degrading treatment. They were a despised lot; even in the middle of the nineteenth century, they suffered *untouchability with a vengeance.*

The caste system of the Tamils, who are mostly Hindus, is also occupation-based. Tamils have high and low caste groups which show a stronger concept of pollution and social distance. At the bottom of the caste hierarchy are three castes of untouchables who suffer social disadvantage more than others. While Pallas and Nalavas (descendants of former slaves) can work on upper-caste land for wages or rent garden land from them, Paraiyars engage mainly in so-called unclean work. While the numerically powerful Vellala or farmer caste is not inclined to loosen its dominant position in society overall other castes.

Recognising that social disadvantages were imposed on people based on the accident of birth or the work they perform, the Prevention of Social Disabilities Act was passed in 1957 and subsequently was amended in 1971 to strengthen its priorities and to impose heavier punishment. The 1978 Constitution prohibits discrimination on the ground of caste (Art. 12 (2)) and prohibits subjecting a person because of his caste to any disadvantage with regard to access to shops, public restaurants, etc., and places of public worship of his own religion. Discrimination based on descent and work may not have disappeared, but there are no signs that it is a problem.

5.2.2

Like India, Nepal has a predominantly Hindu population and a caste system similar to that of India. About 21 percent of the population of 30 million constitute the service castes (untouchables/Dalits) who are engaged in traditional occupations with low status value. They range from artisans and singers to castes doing unclean work like scavenging and removing the dead animal. Despite their significant numbers, they continue to be victimised because of their caste in Nepal, Dalits can and most often are highly excluded from Hindu temples and rituals.

They are also often prohibited from entering hotels, shops or homes, and are even excluded from cowsheds due to the belief that they will pollute the milking cows. In a high profile case in 2000, dubbed the "Gaidakot Milk Scandal" the upper-caste of the Gaidakot Multipurpose Milk Production Co-operative Institution Limited refused to sell milk from an animal raised by a Dalit. Only after protests and the intervention of NGO and human rights organisations, Dalits were allowed to sell their milk to the co-operative.

Unlike India which persistently argues that "the policies of the Indian Government relating to scheduled castes and scheduled tribes do not come under the purview of Article 1 of the Convention on the Elimination of All Forms of Racial Discrimination, CERD., Nepal has provided detailed accounts of the country's problems with caste determination in several of its reports to CERD.

Untouchability was declared illegal in 1963. The Constitution of 1990 guarantees the fundamental rights of the people and makes any discrimination against untouchables punishable by law. While the measures by the state effectively affected the gravity of discrimination, yet untouchability has not been eliminated, that there is an unequal distribution of resources, that many of them remain economically and socially depressed.

5.2.3

In Japan, feudal society lasted till 1867, left a class consisting of eta (extreme filth) and hinin (non-human). The eta was assigned such duties as disposing of dead cattle, leather production, being security guards, and sweeping while hinin made their living as security guards, executioners, and performers. The Buraku, as they are now known, were subjected to intense prejudice and discrimination, forbidden to marry or have physical contact with common people as such contact was seen as "polluting" the higher classes. They were an outcast population.

Beginning with the Emancipation Edict, 1871, many laws have been enacted addressing the Buraku issue. Article 14 of the Constitution of 1946 states: "All people are equal under the law and there shall be no discrimination in political, economic or social relations because of race, creed, sex, social status or family origin." Burakumin "placed in such an inferior position economically, socially and culturally that their fundamental human rights are grossly violated even in present-day society and that, in particular, their civil rights and liberties which are assured to all people as a principle of modern society are not guaranteed in reality". The State took a number of measures to solve the Buraku problem resulting in the improvement of the living standard of Buraku people, but discrimination in marriage and employment continues. Particularly hurtful is the use of derogatory terms in speech and writing.

5.2.4

In Pakistan, Swat is an area of Northern Pakistan that had a system of stratification of unequal social groups (qoum) that can be compared to the Hindu caste system, except that the people are Sunni Muslims. The concept of ritual pollution is absent; its place was taken by notions of privilege and shame. The population of the area is about five lacs and the people are dependent on subsistence agriculture. The groups are such as are to be found in an agricultural community, and at the bottom are despised people – sweepers, washermen, barbers, and those who work with the guts of animals. There is pollution by occupation but caste status by birth does not prevent a change of occupation. In ritual activities there is equality but in everyday situations, a distinction exists. In Sindh Province, about 1.8 million persons are living in bondage as agricultural workers, the majority of whom are Dalits originally from India. A large number of Dalit families work in the brick kiln industry, also under conditions of total bondage.

5.2.5

Dalits in Bangladesh who are originally migrated from India under British rule and remained after the partition of the subcontinent in 1947 work principally as municipal cleaners and domestic workers, lowly jobs that are shunned by the country's majority Muslims, Bengali population. In the country's capital, for example, Dalits make up the majority of the more than five thousand cleaners working for Dhaka City Corporation. They live in small, squalled quarters provided by the city corporation with no gas or electricity.

5.3

Communities outside Asia

5.3.1

The discrimination based on works and descent is not limited to Asia only rather it has a sizeable population in African countries. According to Dr. Rita Izsac-Ndiaye, the former Special Rapporteur on minority issues (2016) there are three types of descent based discriminations in Africa, including caste system based on the occupational specialisation of endogenous groups in which membership is based on ascription and between which social distance is regulated by the concept of pollution and those in which discrimination is based on real or perceived descent from slaves, leaving the fear of reprisals or starvation. Discrimination based on work and descent (DWD) in Africa has been eclipsed by the issue of slavery and child labour.

Slavery and DWD have had a parallel existence for different communities; thus, the former overshadows the latter. The critical feature is that slavery is forced upon a specific community that is socially and economically marginalised. A striking feature is that slavery is linked with inheritance and passed on to generations of the community, thus invoking certain cultural and heritage factors that go beyond pure-economically, motivated norms and behaviours. Children are soft targets for inducing modern forms of slavery, either through the sex trade or through child labour. In Mauritania, Nigeria, Niger, Togo, and Ghana, young boys and girls in trafficking are very common, and often they are from slavery bound communities. However given each of the clear referencing terms, they are often depicted as victims of modern slavery rather than a more expansive notion of DWD. In West African countries the population of these despised groups having different names constitute upto 20 percent of the population of the respective countries. Membership of such groups is based on birth and comprises blacksmiths, potters, musicians, leatherworkers, weavers, barbers, etc. Often they are considered by the majority as being dirty or impure and commonly avoid sharing food with or entering the compounds of members of such groups.

5.3.2

Groups in North-East Africa (the Dime and others)

The literature reveals that a number of populations in North-East Africa, particularly in Southern Ethiopia, exhibit similar features of social organisation and discrimination based on work and descent. The Dime population has a division in pure, non-pure, and impure whose membership is by birth. Endogamy is most strictly observed against the impure groups. The two "pure" groups are considered to have privileged access to the gods and spirits. The polluting propensity of the "impure" groups is quite marked.

Generally regarded as being part of the Borana or Gabre peoples of North-East Africa, the Watta – or Waata Oromo – are a group of (former) hunter-gatherers. Watta groups are scattered throughout Northern Kenya, Central and Western Ethiopia, and the Northern part of the United Republic of Tanzania. The dominant pastoralist communities of the Borana and Gabre tend to marginalise and ostracise the Watta based on their traditional occupational specialisation as hunter-gatherers. Perceptions of the poverty of the Watta are also mixed with attitudes of impurity and pollution. Some elders of the Watta community say that they are considered "impure" by others as a result of their ancestors had hunted and eaten *dirty* animals such as porcupines and tortoises. By way of contrast, the dominant Borana group is known as Borana Gutu (*pure*). A strong social proscription exists against intermarriage with members of the Watta community.

Somali society is described as being divided into patrilineal segmented and ranked clan groups. "*Sab*" is the collective term for "low-caste" occupationally specialised groups within Somali society, known as Midgan (or Madhiban), Tumal and Yibir. Together, the *sab* groups are only a small minority, believed to be less than one percent of the population.

The Tumal are traditionally blacksmiths. The Yibir and Midgan are leather workers. Midgan women also performed female circumcision and acted as midwives to the dominant Somali clans. The occupations of the *sab* groups are generally regarded as polluting, and the members of such groups are consequently considered by other Somalis as having become impure. As a result, intermarriage and commensality between the *sab* groups and the main Somali clans are rare.

In Yemen, the most menial and dirtiest tasks, including garbage collection, street sweeping, and cleaning toilets and drains are performed by Akhdams having a population of more than two lacs. They are widely regarded as being dirty, immoral, and dependent. They rank even lower in Yemeni society than (ex-slaves). They generally live in separate shanty settlements, and intermarriage and socialisation with them are strongly socially proscribed.

In traditional Igbo society, the Osu were ritual servants whose ascribed occupational role was to assist the high priests in the service of the shrines. Osu status was acquired through the ritual transformation of a Diala (*freeborn*) as a punishment for certain offences, by entering the shrine (whether under duress or voluntarily), by contact with an Osu, or by birth to Osu parents. Interactions between Diala and Osu were strictly regulated, out of fear of and respect for the deities the Osu served. Intermarriage, commensality (*inter-dining*), and any other direct contact with an Osu were forbidden. It was also forbidden for a Diala to spill the blood of an Osu. Anyone breaching these rules would themselves become an Osu. Nwaka (1985) records the history of the Osu abolition movement in the 1930s – 1950s, culminating in 1956 in the passage of the *Abolition of Osu System* law by the Eastern Regional House of Assembly (under the colonial administration).

The few available sources emphasise the continuing salience of the stigma acquired by birth into an Osu lineage, or by intermarriage or intimate contact with an Osu descendant.

Dike (2002) places particular emphasis on the continuing *untouchability* of Osu descendants, and the social proscription against intermarriage or sexual relations with an Osu descendant. Dike also describes the political disenfranchisement of Osu descendants and instances of violent attacks against Osu communities.

Recent reports in the popular press in Nigeria also tend to confirm the persistence of prejudice and discrimination against Osu descendants.

5.3.3

Latin America

During the eighteenth century, the growth of sugar plantation caused an increase in the slave trade. The African slaves moved to Brazil and settled with Portuguese, Brazilian aboriginals,

Arabs, and Jews. This escaped group of African slaves organised themselves in a community termed Quilombo initially in Northeastern Brazil. The Quilombos are discriminated against in education, employment, and public services. They often face social exclusion and discrimination because of their colour, skin, and descent and even the end of slavery could not much affect their social condition. The 1988 constitution provided equal rights and protection to all. The Brazilian government has given them rights equal to Brazilian aboriginals and under the "Brazil Quilombola Programme" land titles were given to Quilombos of the land where they lived. The majority of Quilombos live below the poverty line and in a vulnerable position and still have not been integrated with mainstream society.

5.3.4

Europe

During the 1950s to the 1970s, there was a migration wave from South Asian countries to the United Kingdom. The South Asian community carrying their caste distinctions along with them now constitutes an approximate population of 2.5 million. Caste discrimination is quite visible in South Asian society. Some religious groups are mainly from the lowest caste communities, namely Ravidassia, Valmiki, Ramdasis, and Ambedkarite Buddhists. A majority of Christians who have migrated from the Indian subcontinent also belong to the Dalit community. Unofficial estimates put the number of Sikhs in Britain at around five lacs, with one-third traditionally belonging to the Dalit community.

It has been estimated that more than two lacs Dalits live in the UK. Here, untouchability is practised both in the form of direct and indirect discrimination. Discrimination is included in the areas of employment, education and religious institutions, access to goods and services, and particularly concerning access to temples. The more direct forms of discrimination manifest themselves in various types of violence and public harassment. This deeply entrenched form of discrimination is also very much a part of the Diaspora communities in the UK. In the UK, communities, to maintain caste lines, strictly follow the system of arranged marriage. Within caste, marriages have led to the continuation of the caste system within the South Asian diaspora in the UK.

5.3.5

Other countries of Europe

The Romani, also known as the Roma, is an Indo-Aryan people, whose origin is traced back to undivided India, traditionally nomadic living mostly in Europe. They constitute one of the largest minority groups, of around 14 million people. 'It is assumed that the migration of Roma people from India to Europe via Persia, Armenia, and Asia Minor between the 11th and 14th century. Being from the North-west part of the Indian subcontinent, Europeans call them Gypsies because of their mobile lifestyle. Specific anti-Roma racism is termed 'antiziganism', or 'antigypsyism'. They have historically been one of the most vulnerable and most impoverished people who have faced centuries of discrimination in Europe.

People from this community experience high levels of poverty, illiteracy, and unemployment mainly because of the discrimination faced by them in access to education, employment, housing, and health facilities. Roma children are educated in 'special' schools meant for disabled students. There are also widespread incidences of violence against this community. In several European states, Roma people are victims of "ghettoisation", a system wherein the people from this community are made to live in specific parts of towns, away from the rest of the population. The Bulgarian authorities consider "the gravest problem to which Bulgarian Roma are confronted" (according to the Council of Europe) as a "heritage of the past" and not "a deliberate governmental policy.

In certain European states, Roma people are targets of state-sponsored violence. For instance, Roman women, as well as men, are sterilised in several countries since the beginning of the 20th century. Such cases continue to exist even today. In Bulgaria, an informal initiative in January 2012 called for a law that would put in place forced sterilisation of Roma people at birth. State actions of violent evictions, destruction of goods, denial of liberty, and racist attitudes, forced sterilisation, and segregation in public spaces are against the Charter of Fundamental Rights and the Treaty on the European Union.

5.3.6

Rights of Indigenous people

There are around 370 million indigenous people worldwide, living across ninety countries and representing 5000 diverse cultures. They make up less than 5% of humanity, yet represent around 15% of the world's poorest people. Two-thirds of the world's indigenous people live in Asia and the pacific. They include groups often referred to as tribal people, hill – tribes' adivasis, janajati, the aboriginal or native.

Many indigenous peoples remain unprotected and unrecognised. They face forced assimilation, exclusion, and systematic discrimination. Their culture, stories, and knowledge are often deprived of opportunities to fulfil their full potential. The 2030 Agenda for sustainable development promises to ensure a life of dignity for all, having no one behind, so special attention must be paid to the needs and rights of indigenous people.

The International Day of the indigenous people is celebrated every year on 9th August, which is an important opportunity for countries and societies around the world to learn about and commit themselves to the realisation of the rights of indigenous peoples.

5.4

United Nations and Elimination of Discrimination

5.4.1

As the Second World War was about to end in 1945, nations were in ruins, and the world wanted peace. Representatives of fifty countries gathered at the United Nations Conference on International Organisation in San Francisco, California from 25 April to 26 June 1945. They proceeded to draft and sign the U.N. Charter, which created a new International Organisation United Nations which finally began on 24th October 1945. The Preamble of the U.N. envisages to reaffirm faith in fundamental human rights, in the dignity of the human person, and Article 1 of the charter incorporates to achieve international cooperation in solving international problems of an economic, social, cultural, or humanitarian character, and in promoting and encouraging respect for human rights and fundamental freedom for all without distinction as to race, sex, language, or religion.

5.4.2

The Universal Declaration was proclaimed on Human Rights by the United National General Assembly in Paris on 10th December 1948 as a common standard of all people and all nations. It envisages in its preamble, the recognition of the inherent dignity and the equal and inalienable rights of all members of the human family is the foundation of freedom, justice, and peace in the world. Considering that the Charter of the United Nations based on the principles of the dignity and equality, inherent in all human beings, and that all member states have pledged themselves to take joint and separate action in co-operation with the organisation, for the achievement of one of the purposes of the United States which is to promote and encourage universal respect for the observance of human rights and, fundamental freedom for all, without distinction as to race, sex, language or religion and, considering that the Universal Declaration of Human Rights proclaims 'perhaps in most resonant and beautiful words of any International agreement' that all human beings are born free and equal in dignity and rights.

They are endowed with reasons and conscience and should act towards one another in a spirit of brotherhood and that everyone is entitled to all the rights and freedoms set out therein, without distinction of any kind, in particular as to race, colour, or national origin. Desiring to implement the principle embodied in the United Nations Declaration on the Elimination of all the forms of Racial Discrimination and to secure the earliest adoption of practical measures to that end defines racial discrimination in Article 1 which runs as, "racial discrimination shall mean any distinction, exclusion, restriction, or preference based on race, colour, descent or national or ethnic origin which has the purpose or effect of nullifying or impairing the recognition, enjoyment or exercise, on an equal footing, of human rights and fundamental freedoms in the political, economic, social, cultural or any other field of life."

The Human Rights Council in June 2009 has widened the scope of discrimination as," Discrimination based on work and descent is any distinction, exclusion, restriction, or preference based on inherited statuses such as caste, including present or ancestral occupation, family, community or social origin, name, birthplace, place of residence, dialect and accent that has the purpose or effect of nullifying or impairing the recognition, enjoyment, or exercise, on an equal footing, of human rights and fundamental freedoms in the political, economic, social, cultural, or any other field of public life.

This type of discrimination is typically associated with the notion of purity and pollution and practices of untouchability and is deeply rooted in societies and cultures where this discrimination is practised. The council has formulated Draft Principles and Guidelines for the effective elimination of discrimination based on work and descent bearing in mind the commitment to the principles and obligations under the Charter of the United Nations, the Universal Declaration of Human Rights, and the International Convention on the Elimination of all Forms of Discrimination.

Almost all the countries have provisioned in their respective constitutions for the elimination of all types of discrimination and have provided inalienable fundamental rights. The countries have also enacted a number of laws in their respective states depending upon the conditions therein for the upliftment of the people of such disadvantageous class. Several countries have taken very effective affirmative actions like India which has resulted in a significant and distinct improvement in their economic and political spheres. But whatever success we have achieved so far in this regard is limited to only a countable section of the large society. Moreover, the discrimination based on descent and work is changing towards complex and violent forms as we are observing presently. It is the need of the hour that the International community must take vigorous, effective, result-oriented, and specific-targeted measures for the complete dismantling of discrimination based on work and descent.

CHAPTER SIX

HISTORY OF ANNIHILATION OF CASTE

6.1

The existence of the practice of the caste is believed in the Rig-Veda period around 1500 BC wherein it has been delineated in the ninetieth hymn of Purusha Sukta. Although the caste system was not welcomed by the society right from its origin, yet it faced its first challenge only one thousand years later in the sixth century before the Christian era when Buddha recognised the Dalit oppression and felt the need for liberation from this vice. A great revolt against caste was initiated under the guidance of Sakya Muni or Buddha and his disciples, a revolt that became very largely successful over a considerable portion of India. Throughout the whole Buddhist period of India, strong opposition was cherished by the Buddhists against caste. During the dominancy of their religion, which lasted for six or seven hundred year's caste was very depressed, and the people generally enjoyed a condition of social freedom, which they had not since the earliest ages of Hinduism. Buddha's aggressive confrontation with the uncivil social order and compassion for suffering humanity made the untouchables follow Buddhism. Buddhists broke the caste by creating the sanghas that admitted everybody irrespective of the caste they belong to. Yet the caste endured and evolved.

It was the one period of Maurya Rulers in Indian history which is a period of freedom, greatness, and glory. It was the period when the caste system was completely annihilated. The rule of law prevailed over the dharma law. On the fall of the Maurya Dynasty again not only the caste system revived but flourished.

6.2

It is moreover manifest that the Brahmins during the dark night of their own religion, strong to almost to keep alive the flame of the Hinduism and the custom of caste in some parts of the country, despite the gigantic difficulties which at one time they had to face, but the Brahmins are and have ever been among the most persevering, most subtle and most intellectual keen and forcible men that have trodden this earth. And so thwarted baffled, resisted overwhelmed, they never despaired.

Consequently, as their enemies became weak they became strong and were at least victorious because they determined to be. Yet this thousand-year conflict (Buddhist) affords a lesson to the world of what may be achieved by the few against many by a small band of resolute man who prefers their connection to their lives, against a time spirited and multitudinous host, whose strength lies in their numbers, and who through irresolution and bad leadership are unable to make proper use of any power which they may happen to possess.

Thus it came to pass that, with the revival of Hinduism, caste reasserted itself, and stealthily spread over the land as in former times. But its tone, like that of Hinduism, was altered. It has been more arrogant, more tyrannical, more persuasive in its influence, and has held the people with a stronger and more savage grip, than in pre-Buddhist ages. Hindus now cannot marry out of their caste on any pretence whatever. They are tied hand and foot and are a willing slave to the most intolerant and exciting taskmaster that ever placed a yoke on the neck of a man.

6.3

In the twelfth century Ramanuja or Ramanujacharya, a proponent of the Vishishtadvaita gave primacy to Bhakti or worship of a personal god. In his commentary of the Brahma Sutra, he declares the Shudra to be equally fit for studying the Vedas as the Brahmin and is said to have adopted a non-Brahmin as a guru although he himself was a Brahmin. Contemporaneously Basava led the Veerashaiva movement in the Kannada-Speaking South– that launched the literary vachana tradition, repudiated the caste system and the primacy of the Brahmin.

6.4

Next in the fourteenth and fifteenth centuries, saint poets attempted to reform the caste based system and untouchability. The saint poets are called Bhakti Movement poets. Bhakti poets like Kabir, Ravidas, Dadu Dayal and Guru Nanak represented a cultural revolt. Spiritual equality, social justice, and deep sympathy for the common people are major principles of the Bhakti Movement. They also stressed that God is the ultimate symbol of universal level, compassion, and justice. They wished that God should stand on the side of the oppressed, the weak, and the defenceless.

The poetry of the Bhakti Movement is replete with the damnation of caste. Bhakti saints sang songs of towns in timeless places, when untouchables would be liberated from ubiquitous fear, from unimaginable indignity and endless toil on other peoples land. Ravidas spoke of Be-gum-pura, a place with no pain, no taxes or cares… no wrongdoing, worry, terror or torture. In this verse and many others, Ravidas gave voice to lower caste pain at Brahminical society's treatment of them. Like Nanak Dev, he spoke of the casteless society.

For Tukaram, the city was Pandharpur, where everybody was equal, where the headman had to work as hard as everyone else, where people danced and sang and mingled freely. According to Ranade, Tukaram taught that "pride of caste never make any man holy." The Veda and Shashtras have said that for the service of God, castes do not matter, it is God's name that matters, and an outcaste who loves the name of God is very much a Brahmin. David Lorenzen states that the acceptance, efforts, and reform role of Tukaram in the Varakari-Sampraday follow the diverse caste and gender distributions found in Bhakti Movement across India.

Tukaram, of Shudra varna, was one of the nine non-Brahmins of the twenty-one considered a saint in Varakari-Sampraday tradition. Kabir believed in a place of living where everyone lives with love and affection and that place he called Prem Nagar, the city of love. All Bhakti poets-saints believed in the philosophy of a casteless society of equality and brotherhood. They dreamed of the places like Be-gum-pura Pandharpur and PremNagar for their egalitarian society. All opposed the Brahminism which they believed disastrous to the humanity".

6.5

The first radical Dalit protest movement was led by Jyotiba Phule (1827-1890) who fought for the freedom of suppression of a large number of the population who had been facing exploitation and were at a disadvantage in Indian society for the last thousands of years. He struggled to rebuild the society on the matrix of equality, justice, and reason. Phule drew a clear line between the relation of knowledge and power. In this battle against discriminate Brahminism, Mahatma Phule was inspired by the egalitarian philosophy of Buddha and Kabir. Phule believed that education was the source of emancipation and empowerment and therefore he gave maximum importance to education.

Phule himself started schools for untouchable castes and women. He tried to eliminate the stigma of social untouchability surrounding the exploited castes by opening his house and the use of his water well to the members of the exploited castes. He is credited with introducing the word Dalit (broken, crushed) as an ascription of these people who were outside the traditional varna system. On 24th September 1873, Phule formed Satya Sodhak Samaj to focus on the rights of depressed classes such as women, the Shudra, and Dalit. Through this Samaj, opposed idolatry and denounced the caste system. Samaj campaigned for the spread of rational thinking and rejected the need for priests. Phule established Satya Sodhak Samaj with the ideals of human well-being, happiness, unity, equality, and easy religious principles and rituals.

Phule's Gulamgiri (1873) was the revolutionary destruction of the Brahminic culture, the turning point in his life was in 1848 when he attended the wedding of a Brahmin friend. Phule participated in the customary marriage procession but was later rebuked and insulted by his friend's parents for doing that. They told him that he is from an exploited caste, should have had the sense to keep away from that ceremony. The incident profoundly affected Phule on the injustice of the caste system.

6.6

In 1920-1930 Adi-movements emerged as a radicalised attempt by scheduled castes or Dalits or untouchables aiming towards the removal of social evils practice of Indian society which were discriminatory and exploitative in nature. This movement spread across the southern and northern parts of pre-independent India and the areas affected by it were Punjab, Uttar Pradesh, Andhra Pradesh, Karnataka, and Tamilnadu. The emergence of Adi-movements was significant as they were one of the earliest forms of socio-political consciousness put forward by the section of society that never had organised such as long struggle, traces of which can be found in the Dalit Panthers Movement of 1972.

Within this background of evidence of the history of the origin of numerous terminologies to substantiate their subordinate status, Adi-ideology is significant as it bears testament to the earliest assertion of equal rights, humanity and citizenship. The movement stands for a new social order based on equality, liberty and social justice as well as rationalised principles of socio-economic, political, and cultural development of Dalit. It is the movement to regain self-respect and equal status in society. One of the main causes of its emergence was to fight against the evil of practice of untouchability where Dalit were not allowed to enter into temples, public premises, making use of common public resources and denial any kind of social, political, economic, and cultural freedom or equality.

Untouchability was the main social evil of Indian society that discriminates and exploits lower rungs of society.

The movement based on Adi- ideology spread with different names in regions of Uttar Pradesh, Punjab, Andhra Pradesh, Karnataka, and Tamilnadu. In Punjab, it was named Ad-dharam led by Mangoo Ram, Adi-Hindu in Uttar Pradesh led by Achhutanandan, Adi-Andhra, Dravida, and Karnataka in South India led by Bhaghayswam Reddy and Arighayay Ramasawami all indicating claim to nativity and original inhabitants of India. Rashtriya Swayam Sevak Sangh (RSS) in 1920 and the Hindu Mahasabha led to the downfall of the Adi movement. Gandhi's slogan Ram Rajyam and Nehruvian secularism had also caused great destruction to Adi-movements. The fragmented Adi-movements came on to the common platform under the successful leadership of Dr. B. R. Ambedkar.

6.7

Till now untouchables had started realising, protesting, and agitating against the unjust, discrimination, and exploitation being done to them. These depressed classes had started feeling that they are being forced to live in loathsome and abominable conditions of living under the veil of caste system ordained by the divine. The Adi movement successfully germinated the urge for rights of equality and freedom among the untouchables. Desperate with this situation, the reformers had started manoeuvring the people of these despised groups. Gandhi and Tilak called untouchability a disease that was antithetical to Hinduism. In the first, the All India depressed classes conference held in Bombay passed the All-India Anti-Untouchability manifesto.

Dr. B. R. Ambedkar did not attend this conference, although it was presided over by Maharaja Shivajirao Gaekwad, Ambedkar's patron, and mentor. Dr. B. R. Ambedkar believed that it was not just the stigma, the pollution–purity issues around untouchability, but caste itself that had to be dismantled. The real violence of caste was the denial of entitlement to land, to wealth, to knowledge, to equal opportunity (the caste system is the feudal versant of the doctrine of trusteeship: the entitled must be left in possession of their entitlement, and be trusted to use it for the public good.

6.8

In 1924-25 a movement against untouchability and caste discrimination was launched in Kerla popularly known as Viakom Satyagrah. The movement was centred around the Mahadev Temple at Viaokom aiming at securing the freedom of all societies to pass through the public road leading to the Sri Mahadev Temple and was led by a prominent leader of the Ezhava community designated Shudra.

The Lingayat movement started by a Brahmin Vasava in South India also preached against the superiority of the Brahmins, abolition of idol worship, and giving up the caste system.

6.9

The Arya Samaj founded by Swami Dayanand Saraswati (1824-1883) was the first to preach militant Hinduism. It rejected Smriti and Puran, decried polytheism, and accepted the philosophy of one Veda, one Religion, and one God. The Samaj raised its voice against caste and its prohibitions of a sea voyage and started the Sudhi movement or Re-Hinduism the follow- the outcastes, the converts, and other externals. As a proselytising sect, with the great urge for social service, the Arya Samaj is an important factor in the Hindus' resurgence in northern India but now seems to dim a head in the future.

The Ramkrishna Mission represents the synthesis of the ancient or oriental and the modern or western, started ten years after the death of Ramkrishan Parm Hansa by his disciple Swami Vivekanand (1861-1902), it preached that the caste system is for those who are away from God and it should be abolished. It holds up pure Vedantic doctrine as its ideal and aims at the development of the highest spirituality that a man is capable of. Vivekanand's bold proclamation that castes have nothing to do with Hinduism or religion or birth and that Hindu culture and civilisation is the most superior one, had, in fact, astonished the world and infused a refreshing consciousness of inherent strength among Hindus whose attitudes than was marked with a tone of apology and inferiority towards European culture and civilisation.

In Lahore 1922 a militantly anti-caste group of Arya Samaj, the Jat-Pat Todak Mandal (Forum for the Breakup of castes) was founded under the leadership of Bhai Parmanand. Members of this group pledged themselves to a programme of anti-caste propaganda coupled with inter-dining and inter-marriages. The Mandals need to rely on upper-caste Arya Samajis was a persistent problem and eventually broke with the Arya Samaj. Breaking the caste is not an ordinary thing. Even the greatest social reformers have been able to do very little practical work in this direction.

The work which the Mandal has been able to do through inter-caste marriages is not so little as it appears from the surface. The Mandal is not known only for its programmes for eradication of the caste system but more for the invitation to Ambedkar to preside over the conference on caste abolition at Lahore which had to be cancelled due to a dispute on the content of address of Ambedkar which subsequently published as *Annihilation of Caste.* In 1931 the Mandal campaigned against the declaration of castes in the census.

6.10

After Phule's successful contribution in eradicating the sufferings of the untouchables, Dr. B. R. Ambedkar's role is indomitable and unquestionable. Ambedkar stood for the freedom of the Dalits. In 1920 he began the publication of the weekly Mooknayak (leader of silent). He tried to promote education to the untouchables and uplift them. His first organised attempt was his establishment of the central institution "Bhishkrit Hitkarini Sabha", intended to promote education and socio-economic improvement as well as the welfare of the outcastes. By 1927 Dr. B. R. Ambedkar had decided to launch an active movement against untouchability. He began with public movements and marches to open up public water drinking resources.

He also began a struggle for the right to enter Hindu temples. He led a satyagraha in Mahad to fight for the right of an untouchable community to draw water from the main water tank of the town. In a conference in late 1927, Ambedkar publically condemned the classical Hindu text, Manu Smriti, for ideologically justifying caste discrimination and untouchability, and he ceremonially burnt the copies of the text. In1932, the British colonial government on his assertion announced the formation of a separate electorate for the depressed classes in the Communal Award, but later on converted into the reservation of seats in the provisional legislature with the general electorate for these classes on the fierce opposition of Gandhi under Poona Pact.

6.11

As a Chairman of the Drafting Committee of the constitution, the text prepared by him provided constitutional guarantees and protections for a wide range of civil liberties for individual citizens, including freedom of religion, the abolition of untouchability, and the outlawing all forms of discrimination. Ambedkar argued for special social and economic rights for women and won the assembly's support for introducing a system of reservation of jobs in the civil services, schools, and colleges for members of scheduled castes, scheduled tribes, and other backward classes, a system akin to affirmative action. Granville Austin described the constitution drafted by Ambedkar as "first and foremost a social document".

Dr. B. R. Ambedkar fully immersed himself in the task of drafting the Constitution of India, with the single-mindedness of purpose despite the deterioration of health. A speech delivered by Shri T.T.Krishnamachari on 5th November 1948, in the Constituent Assembly shows that Dr. B. R. Ambedkar was in fact the chief architect of our democratic Constitution. In his speech, Shri Krishnamachari drew the attention of the Assembly to the fact that out of the seven members nominated by the Constituent Assembly to the Drafting committee, most of them were not doing the work for one reason or the other and, therefore, ultimately the burden of drafting the constitution fell on Ambedkar.

The majority of India's constitutional provisions are either directly arrived at furthering the aim of social revolution or attempt to foster this revolution by establishing conditions necessary for its achievement." His vision towards society and nation was always pure for either society or nation. Recently the country has fulfiled one of its dreams of one India, one law. He fiercely opposed Article 370 and said," to give consent to this proposal will be a treacherous thing against the interest of India and, I as the law minister of India will never do it. Ambedkar did not reply to any question on it but did participate in other articles. All arguments were done by Krishna Swami Ayyangar.

He wanted the trifurcation of Jammu and Kashmir which now has been bifurcated. He believed in studying from below and thoroughly identified the objecting of Brahmical sacred books. He pointed out that the Hindu sacred books gave higher priority to graded inequality between different classes. They are written to complete the disarmament of the Shudras and the untouchables. Dr. B. R. Ambedkar considered the Buddhist recognition of dignity and equality of human beings and converted himself into a Buddhist. Dr. B. R. Ambedkar recognised in Buddhism an antithesis to discriminatory Brahminism.

6.12

Narayana Guru (1856-1928) born to a family of Ezhava caste, a lower social order caste of Kerala led a reform movement against the injustice in the caste-ridden society in order to promote enlightenment and social equality. He consecrated a piece of rock as an idol of Shiva, when questioned by Brahmins he replied that 'This is not a Brahmin Shiva but an Ezhava Shiva'. It later became a famous quote against casteism. He propagated the motto, One Caste, One Religion, One God for all (Oru Jathi, Oru Matham, Oru Deivam, Manushyanu) which has become popular as a saying in Kerala.

He furthered the non-dualistic philosophy of Adi Sankara by bringing it into practice by adding the concepts of social equality and universal brotherhood. In an all religion conference in 1923, in an effort to counter the religious conversions of the Ezhava community, he displayed a message, "We meet here not to argue and win but to know and be known. After his death, Dharamteertha, born in a Nair family, an ardent follower of Shri Narayana Guru, preached and percolated the messages of his Guru – one caste, one religion, one god – no caste and social egalitarianism.

6.13

Under the influence of the congress and after the death of Dr. B. R. Ambedkar, the Dalit movement split into groups and some of its leaders supported congress and the rest of them remained in the Republic Party of India founded by Ambedkar. Some Dalit educated youths who had been strongly influenced by Dr. Ambedkar came forward to build an organisation in 1972, with the aim of fighting against social problems and the caste system by Nam Deo Dhasal, Arjun Dangle, Raja Dhale, and J. V. Pawar and named it Dalit Panther's movement.

The Marathi word Dalit was propagated by this movement. It did not signify only the untouchables rather used in a wider spectrum of all depressed classes of the society including landless, poor peasants, women, and those who were the victims of all forms of exploitation. They encircled the whole oppressed class under the domain of Dalits. They were inspired by the Black Panthers Party, a socialist and communist political party that sought to combat racial and economic discrimination against African-American, during the civil rights movement in the United States. The Dalit Panthers emerged to fill the vacuum created in Dalit politics resulting from Ambedkar's Republic Party of India splitting into factions. The Dalit Panthers led a huge movement to rename Marathawada University after Dr. B. R. Ambedkar.

Under the influence of Dr. B. R. Ambedkar and in the light of Dalit Panther's movement in Maharastra, Dalit writers initiated the issue of self-respect in their writings. Dalit literature played an important role in establishing social consciousness among its masses. Gradually the awareness spread across India, almost in every region, Dalit writers through their poems, short stories, novels, and autobiographies started questioning the caste hierarchy and political supremacy. Implicitly and explicitly Dr. B. R. Ambedkar's influence on the emerging Dalit writers is very keen and particular. Now Dalit writers aimed at breaking the culture of silence imposed on them. They started telling their stories in their own language and idioms. Now Dalit is an alternative and collective word for Shudras or untouchables or Harijans and a symbol of environment for change, confrontation revolution.

6.14

Mahatma Gandhi's views about caste and the many facets of such social evils underwent a gradual change from the 1920s to the late 1940s.

In 1920 he believed in the inevitable caste system and that the many fruits that Indian society reaped over centuries were mainly owing to this. For example, I believe that caste has saved Hinduism from disintegration. In accepting the fourfold division, I am accepting the law of nature can be quoted.

By mid-20th he vowed to start downplaying the inevitability of natural division. In my conception of the law of Varna, no one is superior to any other – a scavenger has the same status as Brahmin.

As the 30th reached, he started observing that unequal economic and social status perhaps existed, over the ages, and we have to enrich the inheritance left to us and by 1935, caste has to go. The sooner the public opinion abolishes it, the better.

In 1940, he started expressing the importance of marriages between Ati -Shudras and caste Hindus. He accorded higher importance to marriage between Ati-Shudras and caste Hindus by declaring that he will bless a couple if the girl is from another community only.

In 1945 understanding inter-caste as well as inter-religious marriage (if necessary, civil marriages) was a welcome reform, and by 1947 he welcomed inter-religious marriages whenever it took place. Had it not been for his assassination, we would have been witnessing Indian society, move as Gandhi Ji expressed on numerous occasions, entire Hindu society converted to my view.

6.15

Strongly inspired by the philosophy of Ambedkar, Kanshi Ram, a Dalit Government employee, who faced discrimination and humiliation at the workplace became an activist for the cause of the oppressed class in the Seventies. Initially supporting the Republican Party of India soon became disillusioned with its co-operation with the Indian National Congress. In 1971 along with D.K.Khaparde and Dinabhai formed an organisation for the employees of oppressed communities and this became BAMCEF (The All India Backward and Minority Communities Employees Federation) at a convention held in Delhi with an official launch on 6th December 1978, the death anniversary of Ambedkar. The ideology of BAMCEF is to fight the rooted system of inequality that divides Indian society and to abolish the caste system. Surya Kant Waghmore says it appealed to "the class among the Dalits that was comparatively well-off, mostly based in urban areas and, small towns working as government servants and partially alienated from their untouchable identities.

In 1981 Kashi Ram formed another social organisation known as Dalit Shoshit Samaj Sangharsh Smiti (DS4) and in 1984 he founded a political party in the name of Bahujan Samaj Party. He created political awareness among the people of oppressed classes across India and set the agenda of political empowerment of Dalits and consolidated the Dalit voters to achieve it. He was elected as a member of the Lok Sabha. In 2001 he publically announced Mayawati as his successor.

6.16

After the death of Kanshi Ram, Mayawati continued his political party and his legacy of which focuses on social change for Bahujans, more commonly known as Scheduled Castes, Scheduled Tribes, Other Backward Classes as well as converted minorities from these castes. She has been four times Chief Minister of Uttar Pradesh, the largest state of India. As the

Chief Minister, she gained a reputation for efficient governance and promoting law and order. Its tenure as Chief Minister had been for self-rule of oppressed classes and known for bringing Brahmin and Dalits on a common political platform. She is a persistent advocate for the upliftment and welfare of the people at the lowest level of the Hindu social order-Dalits. But she also vehemently never raised her voice for the complete dismantling of the draconian system which is the real root cause of the sufferings of the Dalits for thousands of years.

CHAPTER SEVEN

REASONS FOR ANNIHILATION OF CASTE

7.1

The caste system is not fundamental to Indian society; it is believed to be a distorted form of Chaturvarna, whose origin itself is a riddle. The most believed notion of the origin of Chaturvarna, the Purusha Shukta is also an enigma. Scholars have opined that Purusha Sukta is a later interpolation in Rig-Veda, written long after the close of Rig- Veda. Originally there were only three varnas in the Rig-Vedic society and there is no mention of fourth Varna Shudra anywhere else in Rig-Veda except the Purusha Sukta and which is later interpolation. Moreover, Purusha Sukta, having sixteen verses, is about the origin of the universe, the Indian cosmogony, and verses 11 and 12 describing the Chaturvarna, is the form of society, is neither in consonance with the other fourteen verses nor are of the same significance. This seems that the formation of society has intelligibly been added with the cosmogony, firstly to impress upon the contemporaneous of the Indo-Aryan society form and secondly by comparing the four varnas with different parts of the body having different importance, making hierarchical gradation of varnas by divine order.

Satapatha Brahmana (1000–800 BCE) and Taittiriya Brahmana (400–300 BCE) are equal to Vedas in authority; also describe the three Varna systems of the society. The Apastamba Dharma Sutra (450–350 BCE) describes four varnas Brahmin,

Kshatriya, Vaishya, and Shudra. Among these, each preceding Varna is superior by birth to the one following. The Vashishtha Dharma Sutra (300BCE-100BCE) says there are four castes (Varna) Brahmins, Kshatriyas, Vaishyas, and Shudras. Three castes, Brahmins, Kshatriyas, and Vaishyas are called twice-born.

7.2

Shudra might have been degraded from the second varna to the fourth varna sometime after the writing of the Satapatha Brahmana, wherein there were three varnas and there was no gradation but the four varnas are found in the Apasthamba Dharma sutra along with gradation of inequality. Manu in his Manusmriti, probably written in 184 AD, finally laid law enunciating the ideal of the Purusha Sukta as a part of the divine injunction. He said, "For the prosperity of the world, he (the creator) from his mouth, arms, thighs, and feet created the Brahmins, Kshatriyas, Vaishyas, and the Shudras. The Brahmin, Kshatriyas, and Vaishyas are twice-born castes; but the fourth the Shudra has only one birth. Not only that, he enunciated that Veda is the only and ultimate sanction of Dharma. The original social ideal of Chaturvarna in Purusha Sukta, Manu invested with the degree of divinity and infallibility which it did not have before.

And still, there were four varnas only but subsequently, the gradation of inequality based on different callings spread, the number of castes went on increasing and also the offsprings of inter-caste marriages gave birth to new castes and even upto Manu there were only twenty-eight castes. But the combined effect of different occupations adopted generation by generation, inter-caste marriages, and tribals' conversions to castes, ex-communications by caste councils, upgradation and degradation of castes by Brahmins led to thousands of castes as we have today. But it is a riddle that originally Brahmin was a Varna and still today we have Brahmin as a caste, on the contrary, there was varna as Shudra and we have no caste in the name of Shudra, whereas in this category there are thousands of castes, (now called Scheduled castes). Today no one can claim that he is a descendant of his pure first ancestor on both sides.

Did God also give a certificate while throwing a Brahmin out of the mouth and Shudra out of the feet? Alternatively, did he put a tag for verification to prevent piracy? The most basic document has this feature. Why was god unintelligent enough to miss this? If he was not what method do we have in place to verify whether a person who is claiming to be a Brahmin is indeed a Brahmin? Does he have a DNA certificate that he or she is the biological progeny of the first Brahmin who was spitted out of the mouth of God?

The most ridiculous thing about the birth-based caste system is that it is based on unverifiable words of mouth. There is no way to decipher if Brahmin of today is actually children of Brahmin of yesterdays. Regardless of whatsoever Gotra or Rishi name one may utter, there is no way to test the veracity of the claim. According to Ambedkar," So what if I say that Brahmins (birth based) of today are worse than Shudras because they were born of Chandals around 1000 years ago".

Now pure race exists nowhere and there has been a mixture of all races in all parts of the world. The Brahmin of Punjab is racial of the same stock as the Chamar of Punjab and the Brahmins of Chennai are of the same race as the Pariah of Chennai. The caste system does not demarcate racial division. The castes system is a social division of people of the same race.

7.3

Originally the Indo-Aryan society was divided into three varnas and subsequently on the degradation of Shudra to fourth Varna transformed the society into four classes and this division of society was primarily based on the calling one adopted and could be changed depending upon the occupation one adopts. There are several pieces of evidence of Kshatriyas performing the office of sacrifice and Shudras were the kings. It is the time when the Brahmin started acquiring the privileges for themselves and declaring the superior of all the varnas. And in Manusmriti the Varna system was declared the infallible divine authority and since the degradation of Shudras started and it went on in the most adorable condition to date. Why such a system should continue which is not fundamental, made a divine authority by cleverness to rever one class and adore the other. There is no such system of reverence to one class and abomination to another anywhere in the world and hence India must discontinue it forthwith. In the words of Swami Agnivesh, "Most foolish innovation of evolved human mind, it would be a caste system.

7.4

Man is a social animal, possessing things in common, constituent the society for increasing the sum of human joy and promoting the welfare of mankind. But the parallel activities of the common things do not bind the men in society; the only way by which the man can is by being in communication with one another. Festivals observed by the Hindus are common; they are performed in parallel by different castes and are a hindrance in becoming an integral whole. The caste system prevents common activity, is a barrier to becoming a society with a unified life; and is an antagonist to integrated human happiness. The ultimate objective of all human activities such as the production of things and services, following of customs, framing and obeying rules, enactment of laws, acquiring and providing education, conducting religious and social activities, etc., is for human happiness and the caste system is sworn enemy to it. It seeks to sever natural ties, to alienate friends, to harden the heart, to strife sympathy, to increase pride as self-esteem, to generate misanthropy, to repress the kindly affections, and to destroy confidence and trust, without which society is beset with stings, and becomes a stranger to genuine comfort and peace.

The effect of caste on the ethics of Hindus is simply deplorable. Caste has killed public spirit. Caste has destroyed the sense of charity. Caste has made public opinion impossible. A Hindu public is his caste. His responsibility is only to his caste. His loyalty is restricted only to his caste. Virtue has become caste-ridden and morality has become caste-bound. There is no sympathy for the deserving. There is no appreciation of the meritorious. There is no charity to the needy. Suffering as such calls for no response. There is charity, but it begins with caste and ends with caste. There is sympathy, but not for men of other castes. There is an appreciation of virtue, but only when the man is a fellow caste man. The whole morality is as bad as tribal morality. My caste man, right or wrong my caste man, good or bad. It is not a case of standing by virtue or not standing by vice. It is a case of standing by, or not standing by, caste. Have not

Hindus committed treason against their country in the interest of their castes.

Caste does not result in economic efficiency, caste cannot improve and has not improved race. Caste has, however, done one thing. It has completely disorganised and demoralised the Hindus. Each caste is conscious of its existence. Its survival is the be-all and end-all of its existence. Castes do not even form a federation. A caste has no feeling that it is affiliated to other castes, except when there is a Hindu – Muslim riot. On all other occasions each caste endeavours to segregate itself and to distinguish itself from other castes. There is no Hindu consciousness of kind. In every Hindu, the consciousness that exists is the consciousness of his caste. That is the reason why the Hindu cannot be said to form a society or a nation.

The Hindu religion can not be made a missionary religion until and unless the caste is dismantled. The obstacle in converting to the Hindu religion from other religions is the caste system where to induct the new convert. On the other hand, Hindus from the lower castes scheduled castes and scheduled tribes are venerable to conversions to other religions. The other religions entice the Scheduled Caste and Scheduled Tribes of Hindus to convert to their religions on basis of equal status in the social life of the community in the new religion which is more important. Caste is inconsistent with the conversion from other religions to Hindu.

If we pursue the matter, what enables the Sikh and the Mahomedan to feel so assured and why is the Hindu filled with such despair in the matter of keep and assistance, you will find that the reasons for this difference lie in the difference in their associated mode of living. The associated mode of life practised by the Sikhs and the Mahomdeans produces fellow feeling. The associated mode of life of the Hindu does not. Among Sikhs and Muslims, there is social cement that makes them Bhais. Among Hindus, there is no such cement and one Hindu does not regard another Hindu as his Bhai. This explains why a Sikh says and feels that one Sikh or one Khalsa is equal to Sava Lakh men.

The diagnosis of the fatal disease of the Hindu community was the same as Ambedkar and Jat-Pat Todke Mandal i. e., both were of the opinion that the caste system was the root cause of the disruption and downfall of the Hindus. Dr. B. R. Ambedkar wrote for Scheduled Tribes, "If the savages remain savages, they may not do any harm to the Hindus. But if they are reclaimed by non- Hindus and converted to their father they will swell the ranks of the enemies of the Hindus. If this happens the Hindu will have to thank himself, and his caste system."

The vertical division of Hindu society explains why one Mohmedan is equal to a crowd of Hindus. This difference is undoubtedly a difference due to caste. So long as caste remains, there will be no sanghthan and so long there are no sanghthan the Hindu will remain weak and meek. There cannot be a more derailing system of social organisation than the system which the Hindus are compelled to follow under the guise of shastras. It is the system that deadens, paralyses, and cripples the people from the helpful activity. This is no exaggeration. History bears ample evidence. There is only one period in Indian history that is a period of freedom, greatness, and glory. That is the period of the Maurya Empire.

7.5

Caste is opposed to intellectual freedom. It stereotypes thought. Learned men, professors of colleges, leaders of public opinion, counsellors, judges, magistrates, editors of papers, and a multitude of other persons of talent and education, are bound, hand and foot, by the most childish and insane customs from which, if they deviate by a hair's breadth, they are in danger of ex-communication from the society in which they move, and of which they are ornaments, and of being utterly abandoned by their closest and dearest relatives, as well as by all professed friends.

Caste impedes progress in all facets whether it is an individual's life, society's advancement, advancement in civilisation or national progress. It is the main bottleneck in becoming society wholesome. It hinders the striking out of the new paths and searches for wisdom. Caste not only compromises with each of wisdom, intelligence, justness and even honesty but dominates over all of them. The ties of caste are stronger than any other bond of society, even stronger than the religion for Hindu. A Hindu is more conscious of his caste than his religion where it is reversed in all other religions of the world and resultantly Hindu is not united on religion but his caste. In all the concerns of the Hindu connected with their progress in a very possible way, the great and almost overwhelming obstacle is caste. It fosters jealousness, foments faction, prevents union, and thus represses the natural growth of the nation and keeps it stunned and unfruitful.

Caste is intensely selfish. The object of each separate caste is to seek the welfare of its own small and often insignificant, community, without the least regard to the interests of all others in its neighbourhood. Every caste thinks only of itself, is an empire in itself, is dependent on, the associated with, no other castes cares nothing for any other caste, seeks diligently its own prosperity, and is utterly unmoved by the adversity, which may befall a hundred other castes in its immediate vicinity. A Hindu does not live for himself, but his caste. He will look upon men and women in the utmost distress in perfect callousness when he knows that they do not belong to his caste. This extraordinary and anomalous institution sits like an incubus on the Hindu race. Their social blood has been poised, and their social life has been strangled, by the deadly sting and foul embraces of this serpent. It is impossible that there should be any true and widespread public opinion, or any strong united action, among Hindus, until this monstrous evil has been destroyed.

The anti-social spirits are the worst feature of the caste system. One caste enjoys singing a hymn of hate against another caste. The literature of Hindus is full of caste genealogies in which an attempt is made to give a noble origin of one caste and ignoble origin to other castes. The Sahyadrikhand is a notorious instance of this class of literature. This anti-social spirit is not confined to caste alone but has gone deeper and has poisoned the mutual relation of the subcastes as well.

The Golak Brahmins, Deorukha Brahmin, Harada Brahmins, Palse Brahmins and Chitpavan Brahmin all claim to be sub division of the Brahmin caste. But the anti-social spirit that prevails between them is quite as marked and quite as virulent as the anti-social spirit that prevails between them and non-Brahmins. The Hindus, therefore, are not merely an assortment of caste but are so many warring groups, each living for itself and its selfish ideal. There is another feature of caste which deplorable. The existence of caste and caste consciousness has served to keep the memory of past feuds between caste green and has prevented solidarity.

Brahminism makes it impossible to draw a clear line between victims and oppressors, even though the hierarchy of caste makes it more than clear that they are victims and oppressors. (The line between touchable and untouchable, for example, is dead clear) Brahminism precludes the possibility of social or political solidarity across caste lines. As an administrative system, it is pure genius;" A single spark can light a prairie fire" was Mao Zedong's famous message to his guerrilla army. Perhaps but Brahminism has given us in India a labyrinth instead of a prairie. And the poor little single spark wanders, lost in a warren of four walls. Dr. B. R. Ambedkar said this is the very negation of the spirit of Liberty, Equality, and Fraternity.

One important and very hopeful sign as a presage of the coming reformation is distinctly visible in the strongly expressed wishes of large proportions of the educated and intelligent members of native society. The desire for a radical change, cherished by many of the leaders of Hindu thought, although their number in the aggregate may be comparatively few, is of incalculable value. Such desire is essential before any movement can take place and this is the very class of people who can best of all awaken it in others, and can transmit it to the various grades above and below them. Now in the age of social media campaign for the abolition of the caste system is getting its momentum but it is undirected. A significant section of Indian society is highly feverish to dismantle this notorious system of social stratification, but their delusion is that there is no way which can satisfy their appetite.

7.6

So long as educated Hindus are fascinated by caste notions and customs, their minds will remain stunted and stiff and will reap very little of the most precious fruit that education yields. Caste paralyses the intellect, stifles the soul's generates inspirations, trains the inner eye to gaze on self and nothing else, and perverts the noble end of human knowledge. "Caste restricts opportunity. Restricted opportunity constricts ability, constricted ability further restricts opportunity where caste prevails, opportunity and ability are restricted to ever-narrowing circles of the people" said Ram Manohar Lohia.

Educated Hindus, and all other Hindus who are anxious for their own and their country's progress, will have to move their choice in the matter, either to retain caste and with it all the prejudices, pride barrenness, and mental importance, through which India has been blighted during the dark ages of the past, or to hurl it from them, and cultivating brotherly love towards all men, to regard Hindus of every grade as forming one family or to aim at the elevation and enlightens of high and low, rich and poor, to cherish earnest thoughts for the improvement of the debased and miserable outcastes, so long as neglected and despised as an integral portion of the Hindus family, and thus to feel the glow of hope for their country's freedom from the draconian social system, and for complete deliverance from all the social evils which now oppress it, burning in their breasts.

7.7

Already a struggle between the castes has commenced and is plainly manifest to look on. Knowledge, at all, is no respect of persons and if imparted to all who seek it, the question comes, who will win? In former time knowledge meaning Sanskrit literature, was restricted to the Brahmanical caste, yet that was not the fault of knowledge, but the Brahmins. And now that in this later age knowledge is wider, and at the same time perfectly free, it offers its blessings to whomsoever will accept them. The Brahmin, therefore, or any other caste, has no special privileges. All are equal runners in the race; victory will be to them, not whose lineage is derived for the gods, not who by birth are nobles, princes, and warriors, not whose wealth gives them undue influence and authority but who run the best.

7.8

One of the most hopeful encouraging spans of the times in India is the indisputable fact that principal castes are awakening to life. Previously the Brahmin alone has been distinguished for intelligence. But now, under the multitudinous exacting influences affecting the people generally, they are powerfully moved, and the latent intelligence of a hundred castes is beginning to pierce through the thick mists of dullness which had settled upon them and to shine forth consciously. This welling up, this intellectual revival, this spirit of inquiry visible on all sides are the chief characteristics of the Hindu of our time. It is a most healthy sign.

7.9

In anticipation of this consummation which will be hastened or delayed according to the way Hindus prepares them for it, let them, first of all, believe in their destiny and next determine to remove out of their path whatever interferes with its fulfilment. They have not had an inglorious career, but its brightness has long since faded away. Let them be fully convinced that hope is not lost and that in their own persons they possess the elements of greatness, which need only a fitting opportunity, and the surmounting of opposing influences, to be developed to their fullest extent. Let them resolve to avail themselves of all the branches of knowledge placed within their reading and to submit themselves unreservedly and fearlessly to its plastic and transforming energy.

7.10

As caste is a social distinction dependant on the assumption of an essential and natural among men – a difference by virtue of which one class is accounted pure and another vile, one blessed another cursed, one from head to foot inherently and necessarily good, in every imaginable sense, without blemish or stain of any short, or another utterly abominable and incorrigibly bad – should such a vain assumption continue to be maintained in the face of the intellectual and moral growth of Hindus of all grades, it will infallibly produce fierce strife and animosity among them. Can it be supposed for an instant, that young man of inferior and degraded caste, who by their acquisitions and talents leave all competitors behind them, and under the authority of a liberal and impartial government, vault into commanding positions of trust and honour, will be content to live subject to a social ban, despised and loathed by a proud class of their fellow countrymen, to the brightest and best of whom in capacity, education, virtue, and energy they have shown themselves to be fully equal. Already such men – of such abilities – and such grades – have come to the front.

If the Brahmins, and the upper-caste generally, determine at any caste to continue their reserve and make no approaches toward the lower castes notwithstanding their great improvement in intelligence and knowledge – if they insist on preserving fully and without abatement those social distinctions which were enforced in the dark ages, when nearly all Hindus accept the Brahmins were sunk in ignorance and barbarism, it requires so prophet to foretell that a social rebellion – a caste conversion – is at hand. It is demonstratable, that first as the tyranny of a monarch must fall before the growing liberty of people, and so must caste fall before the increasing enlightenment and progressive civilisation of the Hindus.

7.11

If these statements are true, admitting of no dispute, how important it is that the higher castes should thoroughly understand that great social question, and in a spirit of magnanimity make the first approach towards the lower caste. The growing influence of what may be termed the middle class of native society consists of the Vaishyas, the Kayasths, and the higher grades of Shudras. These are incontestably the most energetic – most pushing and most successful of all the castes and are intelligent, intensely active, and of the immense force of character, some of their members having been educated to the highest point of learning. Let them suddenly arrive at that consciousness – let them suddenly awake the thought that they are as well educated, as able, as intelligent as the Brahmins- are much more successful in their secular schemes- and exert a much deeper and a fare better influence over Hindu society at large; and they can, if they are so inclined, destroy Brahmanism, root, and branch – can utterly annihilate it.

7.12

If the superior castes are wise as well as polite, they will lose no time in holding out the right hand of fellowship to the lower. Such a step would, by its magnanimity secure to them much of the respect and honour which they at present enjoy. The Brahmin would not lose his positions of eminence as the time-honoured leader and instructor of the Hindu race. It is the most baneful, hard-hearted, and cruel social system that could possibly be invented for damming the human race. Furthermore, by patient reflection, he has come to the conviction, that of the superior castes do not presently invent some scheme for its eventual suppression, the inferior caste, when sufficiently educated and thought awakened, will rise in furious and unappeasable indignation and peaceably, though none the less surely, brand them with an indelible stigma of shame.

7.13

Gandhi Ji opined that caste has nothing to do with religion and is harmful both to spiritual and national growth. Varna and Ashrams are institutions which has nothing to do with caste. The laws of Varna teach us that we have each one of us to earn our bread by following the ancestral calling. It necessarily has reference to callings that are conducive to the welfare of humanity and no other. It also follows that there is no calling too low and none too high. All are good, lawful, and absolutely equal in status. The callings of a Brahmin-spiritual teacher- and a scavenger are equal, and their due performance carries equal merit before God and at one time seems to carry identical reward before man.

In 1936, Gandhiji wrote a classic essay called "The Ideal Bhangi" on 28th November in Harijan. The Ideal Bhangi of his conception would be a Brahmin par-excellence, possibly even excel him. The Brahmins duty is to look after the sanitation of the soul, the Bhangi's that of the body of the society – and yet our woebegone Indian society has branded the Bhangi as a social pariah, set him down at the bottom of the scale, held him fit only to receive kicks and abuse, a creature who must subsist on the leavings of the caste people and dwell on the dung heap.

If only we had given due consideration to the status of the Bhangi as equal to that of the Brahmin as in fact and justice he deserves, our villages, no less their inhabitants would have looked a picture of cleanliness and order. I, therefore, make bold to state without any manner of hesitation or doubt that not till the invidious distinction between Brahmin and Bhangi is removed will our society enjoy health, prosperity, and peace and be happy.

Untouchability was born out of the caste system which is a blot on Hindu society. Individual caste solidarity was there but the national solidarity was retarded due to the caste system. Dirks suggested that it was under the British; caste became the single term capable of expressing, organising, and above all systemising India's diverse forms of social identity, community, and organisation. In short, colonialism made caste what it is today.

7.14

Khuswant Singh, the renowned journalist of the popular column, *"Na kahoo se dosti na kahho se bair"*, through his able pen highlighted the abnormal dominancy of some castes in various businesses, professions, and services. Giving the account that Brahmins constituting 3.5 percent of the population of our country hold more than seventy percent of Govt. gazetted posts, more than sixty percent of deputy secretaries, secretaries, and chief secretaries, more than sixty percent of Judges of High Courts and Supreme Cort belong to Brahmins, more than fifty percent the Governors of the states, more than forty percent of Ambassadors, more than seventy percent IAS, more than thirty percent Lok Sabha and Rajya Sabha members. The data is self-explanatory that 3.5 percent of populations of Brahmins hold between thirty to seventy percent of plum government jobs. In the words of Khuswant Singh," How this has come about I do not know. But I can scarcely believe that it is entirely due to the Brahmin higher IQ". The Statistics relate to before 1990. But after the implementation of the Mandal Commission Report, it has changed significantly.

The Centre for the Study of Developing Societies (CSDS) conducted a survey in 2006 for the social profile of New Delhi Media and found that ninety percent of the decision-makers in the English language print media and about eighty percent in television were from upper classes and of them about fifty percent were Brahmins. Not one of them was from Scheduled

Castes and Scheduled Tribes which collectively constituent about twenty-five percent of the total population of India.

The policy of reservation, however minuscule the percentage of the Dalit population it applies to, has nevertheless allowed Dalits to find their way into public services, to become doctors, scholars, writers, judges, policemen, and officers of the civil services. Their numbers are small but the fact that there is some Dalit representation in the echelons of power alters old social equations. It creates situations that were unimaginable even a few decades ago in which say, a Brahmin clerk may have to serve under a Dalit civil servant. Even this tinny opportunity that Dalits have won for themselves washes up against a wall of privileged-caste hostility.

7.15

Violations against Dalit Women and Children

In addition to suffering discrimination based on work and descent, Dalit women and girls also suffer gender discrimination. Women in Dalit communities are poorly educated and subjected to gruelling labour and many forms of violence, including trafficking and prostitution. Dalit women are consistently subjected to physical abuse and sexual exploitation by higher caste landlords. Women are raped, mutilated, and murdered during caste violence. Dalit women do not regularly report incidents of sexual assault because of entrenched biases at every stage of the process.

They have inherited a life of burdens and few rights, a life of continuous discrimination, a life without dignity. The world may have changed around them but not for them. They are, in fact, a race of broken people with commonalities that bring them together. They speak in many tongues but with one voice to ask for social justice and good governance that will end the miseries in their daily lives. They are people subject to violations of their human rights. The strict enforcement of the law can assist the other ongoing educational processes in society to bring about attitudinal changes in the direction of tolerance, compassion, and justice.

7.16

It is highly ridiculous of the Indian society to carry forcefully a system that is perplexing, full of intricacies, and completely unwelcomed since its origin for the last more than three thousand years. Every aspect of this serpent that is stinging the society every moment and infusing the poison into it is itself full of riddles. The first riddle is regarding its timeline of origin. The most believed notion is the origin of the system in the Rig-Vedic period, which is 1500 BCE during which Rig-Veda is believed to be written. One view is that the Chaturvarna system existed during the Rig-Vedic period as found in Purusha Sukta of the tenth book of Rig-Veda.

The other view is that Chaturvarna did not exist during the period Rig-Veda but Purusha Sukta is the later interpolation long after the close of Rig-Veda as Purusha Sukta explaining Indian cosmogony having sixteen verses and verses 11 and 12 are no more than the form of a society divided into Chaturvarna is not at all consistent with the rest of the verses and inducted deliberately. The Sanskrit language of Purusha Sukta is modern and highly improved, whereas the language of the rest of the Rig-Veda is raw and old Sanskrit.

The second riddle is the number of varnas itself. There is no mention of Shudra anywhere else in Rig-Veda other than the Purusha Sukta and later, an interpolation, so originally there were only three varnas Brahmin, Kshatriya and Vaishya found a place in Rig-Veda at several places. Also, Satpatha Brahmana and Tittiriya Brahmana describe only three varnas. These two Brahmanas were written after Rig-Veda and it is evidence that Purusha Sukta was interpolated later even after Satpatha Brahmana and Tittiriya Brahmina were written. This creates an enigma that how four varnas were created when originally there were three.

The third riddle is the origin of the source of Varnas. Vedic, Brahmanas and other Brahminic literature is full of various explanations on the source of Varna and is simply bewildering. Some allege that Purusha was the origin of Varnas and some attribute to Brahma, some to Parjapati, and some to Vartya. Lord Krishna says, "Chaturvamayma mayaa sristam gunkarma vibhagsah." i.e., four orders of society created by me according to their guna (qualities/behaviour) and Karma(profession/ work/efforts).

The fourth riddle is the Gotra itself. In Hindu culture, the term Gotra is considered to be equivalent to lineage. It broadly refers to those who are descendants in an unbroken male line from a common male ancestor or patriline. Panini defines Gotra as "apatyam pautraprabhrti gotram" (IV.1.162), which means the gotra denotes the descendence (or descendants) of a couple consisting of a pautra, a son and a bharti, the mother i.e., the daughter-in-law. Based on Monier Williams Dictionary definitions, when a person says, "I am Vipprala gotra" he means that he traces his descent from the ancient sage Vipparala by unbroken male descent. Many Gotras are found common in different castes.

How a common ancestor having two or more castes is possible? The Chopra Gotra is found in Chamar (scheduled caste), Punjabis and Jats, the Malik gotra is found in Punjabis and Jats, Poonia gotra is found in Chamars (scheduled caste) and Jats and Bisnois, Verma is a gotra which is found in Kumahars (potter), Khati (carpenter), Sunar and Chhipi. Koli is found in Gujjar and Chamar, Kohli is found in Gujjar and Punjabi, Khatana is found in Dhanak and Gujjar. Chauhan gotra is found in Balmikis, the lowest caste in the pyramid of caste, and in Rajputs which is believed to be the descendants of Kshatriya, the second from the top in hierarchy. And the list is not exhaustive.

How common ancestors have more than one caste? No barometer can find, which Verma is Sunar, which one is Kumahar, or which one is Chippi. It's all bewildering and ridiculous. Only one conclusion can be drawn from the gotra concept that the castes are the invention of the ingenious and silly minds.

We are carrying these illusions for thousands of years without any rationality. We have been made to follow it as a divine order and never have questioned ourselves regarding the one major section of our society, how despised and abominable life they are compelled to lead without the fault of theirs.

7.17

The Doctrine of Karma as envisaged in Brahminic literature explains that one takes his birth in a particular caste depending upon his Karma in the previous life and if he abides the caste obligations in the present life he will be promoted in the next life and if he does not follow his caste rules, in next incarnation he will be born in a lower caste. But Lord Krishna does not say guna and Karma of the previous life. In sloka (XVIII.41) Lord Krishna says, "Brahmina Kshatriya, Visham and Sudranam cha paramtapa, karmani pravibhaktani svabhavapra bhavaigunaih." It means people have been grouped into four classes according to their present life Karma (professional/work) and svabhav (behaviour). The division of labour into four categories- Brahmin, Kshatriya, Vaishya, and Shudra- is also based on the gunas inherent in people's nature. Had this division been based on birth, Lord Krishna would have naturally used phrase *Janmani Pravibhaktani* in the very sloka (XVIII.41).

The biological theory explains the four varnas entirely into a different plane that human being inherits three categories of qualities –Sattva, Rajas, and Tamas. The proportion of these categories of qualities differ into four varnas as having the highest proportion of Sattva will be Brahmin and having the highest proportion of tamas will be Shudra.

7.18

It is not only the origin of the source and timeline of the varna that is bewildering and perplexing; the development of caste from varna is also full of more complexities, conjectures and is completely baffling. Historians, sociologists, anthropologists, and other scholars of Brahminic, Vedic, and epic pieces of literature, all have their own theories and explanations and contradict the claims of other's points of view.

Dr. B. R. Ambedkar has said, "Subtler minds and abler pens than mine have been brought to the task of unravelling the mysteries of caste, but unfortunately it remains in the domain of the 'unexplained' not to say of the ununderstood. Never has this observation been social and political life of India is free of its influence. And this influence seems to be on the rise, notwithstanding the best efforts to the category by the state as well as every right-thinking entity."

7.19

Our constitution has provisioned for reservation in government employment and educational institutes for the lower strata of the society who faced social discrimination, economic and political exploitation for thousands of years. This exploitation has affected their mental, physical and economic capabilities adversely from generation to generation. This tool of reservation was employed to bring the left-out untouchables into the mainstream of social life. This has vividly shown its impact on the people who were happy enough to have the opportunity of this privilege, and with the lapse of time and awareness among the people of this section of the society spread the wings in the wider spectrum and the fruits of the reservation policy became sweeter and sweeter.

These positive affirmations have resulted in bringing out a section of our society into the mainstream. But unfortunately, since last three decades these spreading wings had started contracting, one because of the shrinking of the government employement due to the economic reforms initiated by the government of India in 1991[3], being the need of the hour and which continues and will continue in future also in consonance with international economic scenario and exigencies and secondly that section of society which has come out of its adverse conditions for which the reservation was provided, is availing the facility being more capable and competitive to his fellow brotherhood and thereby, the real needy are now left out of this shrinking opportunity.

War for the reservation has already been started, every caste is claiming the reservation, even without applying the rational mind, for which and for how much they are fighting. It has become a source of feuds in society. The Haryana government has provisioned the reservation to the most despised class of the society, the nomadic or Ghumuntu class (who does not have even an inch of land to live in) into the Scheduled Caste category but the other scheduled castes are protesting.

The employment opportunities in government and public sector institutions are a meagre proportion as compared to the corporate and private sectors, where the government cannot enforce the reservation by law. It does not mean that there is no reservation, there is, but of different nature (reservation in government employment is an affirmative action but reservation in private is negative action) which almost bars the entry of scheduled castes and scheduled tribes, particularly in middle and higher echelons of management because of the inbuilt system by default. The appointments are made generally by reference in the corporate sector which promotes cronyism and cronyism is

---

3 Central Government shares in organised sector employment have gradually decreased by 4% from 12.4% in 1994 to 8.5% in 2012 in fifteen years. (prsindia.org/policy/vital-stats/overview-central-government-employees).

built in casteism. All the corporate houses are managed by upper castes, prominently by one caste, the business community, the Vaishya.

The media houses are prominently managed by the Brahmin community. Having a look at the health sector, how many pharmaceutical industries, corporate hospitals, multi-specialities hospitals, individual private hospitals are managed by Scheduled Castes and Scheduled Tribes. Further how many distributors of medicians, medician shops and medical representatives we find from these classes of our society. Decidedly our answer will negativate the opportunities to these categories. I have found a doctor practising in a Multispeciality hospital who has put his nameplate outside his chamber as X.Y.Verma (Sunar). The objective of the doctor is amply explicit. Can a Scheduled Caste doctor put a name plate with his caste and will attract the patients? We all know the answer.

The caste system cannot be allowed to continue further as whatever we have got till now by the positive affirmation will go on declining. And most affected will be the same class which had been suffering for the last thousands of years and will continue to generation by generation. This will be deliberate cruelty on this section of society. We must kill this monstrous as now we can do it and we have facilities and capabilities to do it.

CHAPTER EIGHT

MECHANISM OF ANNIHILATION OF CASTE

8.1

Prevalent social, economic, and political conditions of India necessitate the establishment of an egalitarian society inevitably by completely dismantling the existing caste system in which one fellowman is kept apart from all the rest of mankind by an unnatural divorce in the name of Shudra or Scheduled Caste or Scheduled Tribe. The abolition process calls for multitudinal operations and actions as the system has endless ramifications. The domestic institution not only results in the graded inequality among the castes but adoration and venerations for one caste; an abomination and abhorrence for the lowest in the scale.

The lower castes Shudras, now called Scheduled Castes and aboriginal tribes called Scheduled Tribes not only had a loathsome and oppressive living but kept devoid of acquiring of knowledge, leaving no option of respectful avocation for livelihood to save menial labour and the mercy of Savarnas, since the acquiring of this monstrous form of the social system and more disastrously after the code of Manu and subsequently Samhitas and Commentaries on Upanishdas and Puranas. Revolt against this monstrous vice paid no dividends in the past. Nevertheless, the aggressive, ferocious, and persistent efforts of Ambedkar and constitutional provisions diluted some of the attributes of the caste system but the system itself not only lively exists but flourishing in different new dimensions which have become the cause of bane in the integration of not only of the nation but of Hindu religion also.

Our revered and venerated saints, social reformers, philosophers, and socio-political leaders realising the deleterious effects of the caste system, had adopted their path to demolish it, not finding possible success to kill the monstrous, parted ways for the formation of an egalitarian world of their imagination. The Gautam Buddha, Guru Nanak Dev, Saint Kabir, and Swami Dayanand formed their sects based on equality and fraternity. Later Jyotiba Phule revolted against the caste system ferociously and struggled against the caste system being within the system itself, although unsuccessful in dismantling the caste system, yet could be successful in realising the oppressed and despised people about the injustice done to them, is not of divine but the product of the society only and which must go. Dr.B.R.Ambedkar came out of the system when disillusioned completely, and renounced the Hindu religion, and joined Buddhism just a few months before his death after a long waiting of more than twenty years since the declaration of renunciation of Hindu religion.

All our venerated leaders were against the caste system and fought tooth and nail for an egalitarian society, the spirit of our constitution is also for the establishment of the egalitarian society with the three attributes provided by Ambedkar known as trinity equality, liberty, and fraternity, but instead of natural death of caste system, it is flourishing with the increased intensity of enmity among the various caste groups. It is manifest that the effects of honest efforts failed, it must have some cause based on the doctrine of cause and effect. The effect is manifest; the cause has to be traced out.

In the voyage of tracing the causes for unsuccessful honest and dedicated efforts, it takes me in two different dimensions supplementary and complementary to each other in two time periods. In the first place, the reformers working for the dismantling the monstrous system, had the tool for it of spiritual knowledge, moral value, the principle of equality, and brotherhood. Their teachings affected the people efficaciously but a few, as forces in favour of propagating the system, were more powerful and people were ingeniously tied in the yoke of Karma. The other factors feeling of pride, having privileges, and conferring power upon the caste below it on the hierarchical scale along with wonderful fascination and authority helped the system impregnable on a social scale. The first cause I find that those reformers, despite having selfless, positive, and powerful social reforms, lacked the backing of force of law.

In the second place, I move to the post-independence era, the constitution made many affirmative provisions for the welfare and upliftment of the depressed and despised section of the society, particularly the Scheduled Castes and Scheduled Tribes who led an abominable, loathsome and oppressive life for thousands of years. The provision of Abolition of Untouchability has made a considerable dent in the immobility of society. The sole intent of the constitution is the formation of an egalitarian society, nevertheless, the caste system not only remains intact but entrenched and modernised.

The legislators take oath for upholding the constitution, had never uttered a single word on the abolition of this disastrous institution of graded inequality; rather it is used as a means of transport in the journey to the legislative houses. Despite having effective and expressive provisions in the constitution, legislature having unfettered power for enacting laws for the welfare of Scheduled Castes and Scheduled Tribes; even after a lapse of more than seventy years, the core issue of the egalitarian society, the dream of our founding fathers, remained unnoticed. Here in the venture, I find that having legal provisions, power to enact the laws for abolishing the caste system, but has remained devoid of the raising a voice for social reforms and support helped the system to perpetuate.

Looking into the past, no social reform could take place unless it had legal sanction, be it Child Marriage, Sati Partha, Untouchability, and such others. Social reforms can not be enforced without legal sanctions and law can not be implemented without the support and involvement of society. Social reforms and force of law are supplementary and complementary to each other. The dissolution of the present system of social stratification having graded inequality is the need of the hour. It is a great threat to the integrity of the nation, social, cultural, and political harmony. The egalitarian society will not only make the nation stronger but will bring the group belonging to the bottom of the caste pyramid equal to the belonging to the top of the pyramid by social osmosis resulting in swimming in the same pool, sailing in the same boat, playing music like Laxmi Kant and Pyare Lal, singing chorus like Mukesh and Mahinder Kapoor, worshipping the same God at one point of time and one place and performing ceremonial rituals for each other.

8.2

Constitutional Amendments

As foresaid complete annihilation of Caste cannot be achieved without the force of law. Certain constitutional amendments and legislative enactments will help to achieve the objective of a casteless society. Some of them may be:

Constitutional Amendments

1. Amendment in Article 17[4]

In Article 17 the word "and Casteism" may be added after the word Untouchability. The Untouchability is born out of casteism and hence the abolition of Casteism is a condition precedent to the abolition of Untouchability.

2. Amendment in Article 18

Clause (5) may be added in Article 18 abolishing the surnames such as subcastes, gotras, or any other title which allude to any caste as per the requirement of the law.

Ambedkar thought of the constitution as a work in progress. Like Thomas Jefferson, he believed that unless every generation had the right to create a new constitution for itself, the earth would belong to the dead and not the living.

---

4 Ambedkar said,"Some men may say that this should be satisfied with the abolition of untouchability only, leave the caste system alive. The aim of abolishing untouchability alone without trying to abolish the inequalities inherent in caste system is a very low aim. Let us remember, "not failure but low aim is a crime." Let us probe the evil to its very roots and be not satisfied with palliatives to assuage our pain. If the disease is not rightly diagonised, the remedy will be useless and the cure may be postponed". (BAWS V-17(1) 62, Low Aim is A Crime)

8.3

Legislative Enactments

The law may be enacted affecting the Annihilation of Caste providing that:

1. All castes of General Category be assimilated into one class, maybe called General Category, and all individual castes stand dissolved.

2. All castes of Other Backward Classes stand dissolved and are assimilated into the General Category.

3. All individual castes in the Scheduled Castes Category stands dissolved and only one single Category be created for all the dissolved castes of Scheduled Castes and may be named General Category (Special)

4. All individual tribes in the Scheduled Tribes may be dissolved and only one category of Scheduled Tribe be maintained and be included in General Category (Special)

5. Those Scheduled Castes and Scheduled Tribes are serving in Group A and Group B services of Central Govt., State Govt., Banks, Insurance companies, Public Sector Undertakings, and other organisations may directly be assimilated into the General Category either voluntarily or by law. All those private-sector employees and businessmen who are in parity with the aforesaid category also be shifted to General Category.

6. Those Ex-employees of Group A and Group B who are drawing a certain amount of pension or having any child employed additionally in Group A or Group B or Group C be also included in the General Category.

7. All M.Ps, M.L.As, and M.LCs of Scheduled Castes and Scheduled Tribes are directly shifted to General Category. Ex-Ministers, Ex-M.Ps, Ex-M.L.As, and Ex-M.L.Cs and any others who are drawing a pension of a certain amount or more are directly shifted to General Category.

8. Those that are willing to shift to General Category from Scheduled Castes or Scheduled Tribes be affected.

9. Any such other justified parameter is made to achieve the objective of a casteless society.

8.4

Assimilation of General Category (Special) into General Category

The Scheduled Castes earlier known as Shudras and to whom Ambedkar had called Untouchables, Unapproachables, and Unseeables, had been suffering from immense discrimination, living with the stigma of abject outcastes, with a treatment of detestation, completely on the mercy of Savarnas for their bare necessities, even of food for survival, subjected to continually meanly paid or begging, forced labour, prohibited to learn and listen Vedas in Vedic period, debarred from acquiring knowledge in later Vedic and Brahmana period and ultimately circumstances forced them to be devoid of education and thereby till Independence remained in pitiable and abominable condition for whom leading a civilised decent life was not even a dream save the Maurya and Ambedkar period.

In such circumstances, who had been such sufferings, oppressiveness and subjected to slavery for thousands of years from generation to generation are not only incompatible to assimilate immediately with the General Category, but it will also be a further injustice, without effective and efficacious affirmative support measures, save who acquired privileged position since independence.

It is distinctly evident that social and cultural environment, economic conditions are the major attributes that affect the physical and neurological development and growth of a man since his birth (even in conception stage)[5], and Scheduled Castes and Scheduled Tribes had been devoid of the favourable conditions to their development of their person at parity with the upper castes for thousands of years. If still allowed the prevailing conditions, resulting the present generation and several future generations will have to wait for the sweet taste of civilisation and till then will remain in the abominable and abhorrent conditions.

It will be a grave injustice to these classes in the present time if they are not provided with the opportunity for their contribution to forming an egalitarian society. Therefore, it is the prime duty

---

5   At certain seasons of the year, the turtle comes in from the sea to deposit their eggs on tropical branches, they return to the sea immediately, leaving their eggs to hatch in due time from the heat of the sun. Eventually, the little turtles emerge from the shells, push up through the warm sand, and head for the sea. They are guided by a sure instinct and without any need for instruction or learning, they take care of themselves, seeking food where it may be found and avoiding the dangers which are everywhere. These turtles grow up without learning or instructions because their nervous system is connected up and functioning as soon as they emerge from the shells. The newly hatched turtle is not so much immature as a small turtle. Living things that can care for themselves in this way and for this reason, are not unfamiliar. Insects do so and to do such animals as chicks and ducklings.

But man is constructed on an entirely different plane. When a baby is born, it is quite incapable of taking care of it and remains relatively helpless for years. Indeed, it would seem that twenty or more years are necessary before a human being reaches maturity. (The Evolution of Civilisations By Carroll Quigley)

of all the privileged class and the state for bringing out them from the conditions in which they had been living for ages and make them compatible with the privileged and upper-caste of society without further waiting.

To bring them at parity with upper castes, in addition to other effective measures described ahead in the following pages, the first and for most is, sufficient economic support, without which all others will result in a futile exercise. For this, all the unprivileged Scheduled Caste and Scheduled Tribe households should be provided the monetary support of Rupees three thousand per member of the family to the maximum of Rupees fifteen thousand per month for the next ten years along with wheat and rice being provided as of today. The monetary support to continue till the family earns, aggregating with his own calling Rupees twenty-five thousand or Rupees five thousand per member and thereafter be apportioned accordingly.

This monetary support should be given in name of the women member of the family enabling women empowerment. The prevailing reservation policy for the Scheduled Castes and Scheduled Tribes be continued for another ten years and those during the continuance of the scheme who acquires the privileged position, be included in the General Category. The two mandatory conditions for availing of the scheme to be, one, the two children policy[6] and the second all eligible children

---

6 B. R Ambedkar believed excessive growth of population is the major cause of poverty. The Scheduled Caste Federation under the Chairmanship of Ambedkar on October 6, 1951 in its manifesto proposed to fight the battle against poverty. For reducing the population, it would advocate intensive propaganda in favour of birth control among the people. It will advocate the opening of birth control clinics in different parts of the country. It regards the growth rate in the increase of population in the country so grave an evil that it would not hesitate to advocate more drastic methods of controlling it. (BAWS. Vol 17(1) 432 Problem of Poverty.)

must get the education upto 10+2 or 10+skill development programme. Once they start getting the scheme, they may be called General Category (special) instead of Scheduled Caste and Scheduled Tribe. And on the completion of the scheme, or otherwise compatible to be promoted in between, be promoted to General Category, forming the egalitarian society and fulfiling the dream of our founding fathers and a tribute to who sacrificed their lives for the freedom of our country.

8.5

Monetary Support Scheme

The first general census of India was done in 1881. It was at the census of 1891 that an attempt to classify the population based on caste and race and grade was made by the Census Commissioner of India. Attempts to make the census based on the castes were made in the subsequent enumerations but it was the census of 1931 which able to state with some degree of surety that the population of untouchables in British India was 44.5 million.

The first post-independent India census of 1951 gives the population of Scheduled Castes in India as 513 lacs out of the total population of 3567 lacs. The census of 2011 having a total population of 121 cr having a population of Scheduled Caste is twenty cr which is 16.6% and that of scheduled tribes 10.5 cr which 8.6%. The present estimated population of India is 135 cr, assuming the same percentage of Scheduled Castes as 16.6% and that of Scheduled Tribes as 8.6% makes 21.9 cr and 11.3 respectively and aggregating to 33.2 cr of both categories.

Indian families comprising five members resulting in 6.64 cr households of combined Scheduled castes and

Scheduled Tribes. Assuming thirty percent of families have come to self-sustainable level in seventy-five years and may well be kept out of monetary support, leaving the beneficiaries as 4.63 cr requiring an amount of 69450 cr per month resulting in 833400 cr annually. Assuming a contribution of 70:30 of centre and states, their respective contribution comes out to be Rs.583380 cr and 250020 cr. These are the guiding principles only, the actual scheme and amount may vary at the time of implementation depending upon the actual data and scheme exposure.

8.6

Financial Implications

The total sum required will be about six percent of GDP, whose arrangement from the economy of having the highest growth potential will not be much tough affair, even without affecting the other areas, some of the possible ways are as follows:

1. A large sum of amount is currently provided to these unprivileged and oppressive classes of the society by the central and state government. All such schemes may be merged with the monetary support scheme such as Manrega, Mid-day meal, Gas, Kerosene and electricity subsidy, education allowance, scholarships and such other schemes which are run by the central or state Govt. especially for these classes to give monetary support.

2. MPs and MLAs Local Area Development Fund may be utilised for the next ten years for this purpose either by respective Govt. or the MPs and MLAs may adopt

the families through the District Nodal officers to be appointed for implementation of the scheme.

3. The remuneration, perks, and pensions payable to the MPs and MLAs had always been a matter of controversy. All these take oath in the name of upholding the constitution which envisages an egalitarian society. To contribute to the noble cause 10 percent of their salary or pension and 20 percent of each who has more than one member of the family may be easily made. This will not be only a financial contribution but practical participation in the noble cause of the formation of an egalitarian society.

4. A cess per litre on petrol and diesel will not be difficult for the cause.

5. Corporate Social Responsibility Fund:

The Companies Act 2013 provides 2% of the net profit for CSR for the eligible companies, it may be increased to 3% for ten years, and also 1% may be provisioned on other companies presently not eligible on some revised criteria. All such funds are used for this scheme either by Central Govt. or the companies may adopt the families through the nodal officers.

6. Contribution from NGOs:

The funds of all NGOs be utilised for the next ten years for this scheme either by Central Govt. or the NGOs may adopt families through the nodal officers.

7. Voluntary contributions by individuals, social organisations, associations, business houses, etc., may be encouraged.

8. India is proud of having a large number of philanthropists in the world, they may work as the driving force for achieving our objective of an egalitarian society.

8.7

Reservation Policy

1. The reservation policy in employment and education for the General Category (special) presently Scheduled Castes and Scheduled Tribes must continue in the present form by adopting the policy of converting from General Category (special) to General Category who becomes eligible.

2. The present reservation policy for other backward classes is changed to an economic basis for the whole General Category and the creamy layer is brought down lower so that the real needy get the benefit of it.

3. Those who get admission through reservation in IITs, IIMs, IIITs, NITs and AIIMS, and such other institutes must not take the benefit of reservation in services and be left to other eligible fellows.

4. On completion of ten years of this reservation policy, afterward completely may be changed to economic criteria on the formation of an egalitarian society.

8.8

Factor favouring to the abolition of caste system

The three factors, Swachh Bharat, Housing for all, and health insurance scheme Ayushman Bharat are not only favourable but will prove to be helpful in the abolition of caste and implementation of Monetary Support Scheme.

Swachh Bharat movement's role in the abolition of the caste system will be a milestone. Manual scavenging has become the thing of the past. The cleaning and manual scavenging were mainly done by Balmikis, Bhangis, and such other castes named differently in different geographical regions. Mahatma Gandhi had placed Balmiki and Brahmin on equal footing as both are the ambassadors of cleaning, one for physical and the other for soul. Narender Modi (Prime Minister of India) has washed the charans(feet) of five warriors of Swachh Bharat. It was not symbolic but regard was accorded to the dignity of labour.

Housing for all as planned by the seventy-fifth independence anniversary will prove to be a stepping stone in removing the inequality in the society and the confidence building of the lower strata of society. To have a roof of own on one's head is a lifetime dream of everyone irrespective of any class, creed, gender, or religion and whatever different attribute for stratification of a society we may choose.

Health insurance for all under Ayushman Bharat is another area that will benefit most of the downtrodden people of our society. Because presently these remain devoid of better health facility of treatment and, on the treatment they had to spend beyond their capacity and was the main hindrance in improving their socio-economic condition. The expenses on the illness of the poor never allowed him to come out of poverty. This health scheme not only will help in physical and economic health but his mental health will get a boost and will improve substantially which ultimately will contribute to the progress of the nation.

A considerable body of evidence has established that individuals of low socio-economic status are more likely to suffer from the disease, to experience loss of functioning, to be cognitively and physically impaired, and to experience higher mortality.

8.9

Implementation of Annihilation of Caste

The monstrous caste system cannot be killed with only one weapon of the Monetary Support Scheme. It has to be pierced minutely on every part of it which has deeply penetrated in our society in every sphere, in tangible or intangible form. This horrible abominable social system of thousands of years old with thousands of ramifications and roots has to be destroyed and uprooted completely leaving no iota of survival or revival.

8.9.1

Role of political parties

All political parties must include in all bodies right from bottom to top at least twenty-five percent from the General Category (special) preferably from the lowest category of Balmikis, Bhangis, and such other castes. And at every alternate term, the President of the party be appointed from the General Category (special) which further may be selected alternatively from earlier Scheduled Caste and Scheduled Tribes for the next fifteen years.

8.9.2

Role of MPs, MLAs, and MLCs, etc.

All MPs, MLAs, and MLCs must voluntarily relinquish their status of Scheduled Castes, Scheduled tribes, and Other

Backward Class and opt for the General Category so that further opportunity is available to unprivileged and left out people of these classes since independence.

8.9.3

Role of Professionals, Businessman, and Employees

All Grade A and Grade B SC, ST employees of central and state governments, PSUs, Banks and such other institutions; professionals like engineers, doctors, advocates etc.; businessmen and industrialists should voluntarily opt for General Category.

8.9.4

Role of Hindu Religious Bodies

There is one grey area where the Scheduled Castes and Scheduled Tribes have been kept away and that is in the management of temples and in officiating priesthood. The act of not allowing a class of people for praying to the God or Goddess is a curse on humanity*. All the social organisations like RSS, VHP, Arya Samaj, and such other bodies train at least one lac people for the priesthood in the temples and the ceremonial and ritual functions from the Scheduled Castes and Scheduled Tribes and particularly from the Balmiki in Haryana, Bhangi in Gujrat and Punjab, the Pakhis in Andhra Pradesh, and the Sikkaliars in Tamilnadu and such other categories preferably[7]. On acquiring such knowledge and competency, twenty-five percent of such trained personnel from these categories be employed in all the

---

7 In 1950 Iyer Commission had recommended to set up a central institution for the training of priesthood and ceremonial rites.

positions of temples right from bottom to top including the chief priest and managing trusts for fifteen years. As the construction of Ram Mandir is in progress, the trust itself must train the required personnel so that on opening for the public, these persons find themselves their place, and the real foundation of Ram Rajya is laid down. It is a universal belief that all are equal before God. All ritual and ceremonial rites literature and hymns are translated into vernacular.

8.9.5

Scheme for Home coming

Every nation has a culture and place in history. The citizens of the nations also have loyalty towards their nation's culture. People's respect towards a nation's culture helps to strengthen the nation itself. Indians consider their nation as their motherland. A religiously converted man loses loyalty and respect towards the nation's culture. Noble laureate V.S.Naipaul in 'Beyond Belief' has written that "A man who has undergone a religious conversion, loses his own past. For him his heritage and culture of his ancestors are meaningless."[8]

There is ample evidence in history that Mughals have forcibly converted Hindus to Islam. Those Scheduled Castes and Scheduled Tribes either who are forcibly converted, or enticed by other religions to convert or converted voluntarly because of persecution by higher castes and are willing to come back to join their heritage and culture of their ancestors, should be included in the category of General Category (special) if they were from the Scheduled Caste and Scheduled Tribes, and in the

---

8   Hardyanaryan Dixit, Dainik Jagran 20th September2020

General Category if they were other than Scheduled Castes and Scheduled Tribes because it was not their fault but of the system itself and circumstances.

8.9.6

Role of Media Houses

This is another area where this despised and oppressive group completely appears to have been ignored. Both electronic and print media houses must provide the training to the people of these groups and on acquiring the required competency must engage at least twenty-five percent in each category including the management for fifteen years. This role of media will prove to be the highest contributing towards transforming society into an egalitarian society.

8.9.7

Change of Names and Titles not alluding to caste

All individuals should replace the gotra after their name with the titles like Bharti, Bhartiya, Arya, Profession, place of birth, and so on of one's choice. If no one changes himself, the name of the father is added by default.

All the names of institutions, associations, body corporates, business entities, professionals should change their names in such a way that no indication of any caste is found.

8.9.8

Change in the PDS system

After having the housing for all, by providing the containers on a cost basis, the wheat and rice may be distributed for six months. It will reduce the storage and logistic cost as well as increase the storage capacity for food grains.

8.9.9

Abolition of Scheduled Caste, Scheduled Tribe, and Backward Class commissions

The abolition of the caste system will result in abolishing the Schedule caste, Scheduled Tribe, and Backward Class commissions, and the monitoring of the scheme may be supervised by creating a department in the Ministry of Social and Justice through the nodal officers at the District level.

8.9.10

Abolition of Legislative Councils of States and Legislative Assembly of Delhi

In the changed contemporary circumstances presently there seems no necessity of the Legislative councils of the states and it is causing the only burden on the exchequer, their abolition will be a right step and fulfiling the principle of minimum government and maximum governance. Also, there has been a controversy among three organs of administration of Delhi, Delhi Govt., Municipal corporations, and Central Govt. The Delhi state can not hold the status of a full state being the capital of the country, and hence it will not be inappropriate to make it union territory without legislature as it was earlier.

8.10

History of Movements in India

The reminiscences of the epoch revolution of 1857 turn the faces red even of eighty years old person even today, are infusing new blood for participating in any such other movement. The bravery of Rani Laxmi Bai of Jhansi is found nowhere in the world. Thousands of people sacrificed their lives on the call of Rani for the nation.

Shaheed Bhagat Singh, Rajguru, and Sukhdev were in high pride and morale while they were hanged. For them, this voyage of freedom for the beloved nation was no less than a pilgrimage.

Neta Ji Subhash Chander Bose's call," You give me your blood and I shall give you freedom." On one call thousands of people offered their sacrifice and joined the Indian National Army, the real hero of freedom of India.

Gautam Buddha, Guru Nanak Dev, Saint Kabir, Swami Dayanand, and Swami Vivekanand were the religious and social leaders who always thought of mankind and humanity. Thousands of lacs of their following indicate their selfless devotion to the service of mankind.

Dr. B.R.Ambedkar's movement against the thousands of years of discrimination and oppression of untouchability and forming a society on the principle of the trinity of liberty, equality, and fraternity is found nowhere in the world. He successfully laid the foundation of his dream of egalitarian society by incorporating several provisions in the constitution being the Chairman of the Drafting Committee of Constituent Assembly.

During the 1965 war with Pakistan, the then Prime Minister Lal Bahadur Shastri's call for one day fast in a week was enthusiastically adopted by the whole of India. His slogan Jai Jawan, Jai Kisan infused the new blood of pride not only in the communities for which it addressed but for the whole of India.

Lok Nayak Jai Parkash Naryan's movement popularly known as JPs Movement against the draconian laws suppressing democratic and fundamental rights was ever largest movement in terms of people's participation.

Anna Hazare's movement against corruption and Mahatma Gandhi's Satyagrah movement where people's participation made the movement successful resulting in the Governments of the day, out of power. Even in present times, the two movements of Swachh Bharat and Jan Dhan Yojna bank accounts are most successful because of people's participation.

While resigning from the government service, Kanshi Ram declared that he will dedicate his entire life for the causes of community, will never get married, will never acquire any property, will never visit his home, and will devote and dedicate the rest of his life to achieve the goals of Phule and Ambedkar movement.

All the aforesaid movements transformed into their desired goals and objectives are the result of people's participation in the movements because the objectives were pure of a noble cause and whose leaders were ready for any sacrifice ahead of people of their movement.

The abolition of caste is that noble cause that will not only transform the social structure of our country but simultaneously reinforce the integrity and strength of our country's manifold. The objectives are directed towards the formation of an egalitarian society, and in real terms, is another freedom movement, earlier it was for political freedom and this one is for social freedom. And this will not be limited to our country only but a path showing to the whole world and ultimately whole humanity will be benefited.

Ambedkar for the Real Service to the Nation-states, "Ours is a movement which aims at not only removing our disabilities but also at bringing about a social revolution, a revolution that will remove all man-made barriers of caste by providing equal opportunities to all to rise to the highest position and making no distinction between man and man so far as civic rights are concerned. If we achieve success in our movement to unite all the Hindus in a single caste we shall have rendered the greatest service to the Indian nation in general and to the Hindu community in particular. The present caste system with its invidious distinctions and unjust dispensation is one of the greatest sources of our communal and national weaknesses."

Generations ago the American poet James Rossell Lowell has written on self-determination which is now quite relevant to India regarding the abolition of the caste system, a cruellest system of social stratification for humanity.

Once to every man and nation comes the moment to decide,

In the strife of truth and falsehood for the good or evil side;

India is full of the most innovative brains; immense vitality, highest unexplored economic and human resources, and all collectively shall dismantle the caste system. Acknowledging Ambedkar, "you must make your efforts to uproot caste, if not in my way, then in your way." Humanity is in the blood of India as a nation and Hindu as a religion.

Our society should be identified by the seawater not the water of different caste rivers. As all rivers having different water but after submerging into the sea, it becomes seawater only, similarly on dismantling all castes, people belonging to different caste will be assimilated whole in one society and will be identified by only Indian society.

REFERENCES

CHAPTER 1

1. Report On Backward Class Commission by Sh. B.P. Mandal

2. Recent Services Journal 1993 (1) SC 7 Indira Sawhney and Ors Verses Union of India and Ors

CHAPTER 2

1. Dutt, N.K.,Origin and Growth of Castes in India

2. Recent Services Journal 1993 (1) SC 7 Indira Sawhney and Ors Verses Union of India and Ors

3. Ambedkar, B.R., BAWS Vol. 1Castes in India

4. Ahuja, Ram., Indian Social System

5. Baba Saheb ambedkar Writtings and Speeches (BAWS) Volume -7

6. Pandey.S.Manali., History of Indian Caste System and its impact on India today

7. Sherring, M.A., Hindu and Tribes of Castes , Trübner & Co. London Volume 3

8. Sociology discussion.com/caste/7-major theories/2354

9. BAWS Vol-1

10. Mondal,Puja.,yourarticlelibrary.com/sociology/differencebetween-class and caste

11. Murdoch, Johan., Caste:its suppositionorigin:its history:its effects,the duty of the government,Hindus and Christians with respect to it; and its prospectus

CHAPTER 3

1. Quigley,Carroll., The Evolution of civilisation

2. Ahija, Ram., Indian Social System , Rawat Publications

3. Beteille, Andre,Castes: Old and Neaws, Essay in Social stratification

4. Ghurye,G.S.,class and occupation,Popular Book Depot , Bombay

5. Gould,Garold, The Hindu Caste System , Chankya Publications, New Delhi

6. Betelie,Andre, Cast, Class and Power, California University,Berkley

7. Dumont, Louis,HomeoHierachicus, University of Chicago Press, Chicago

8. Gould, Harold, Caste adaptation in Modernising Indian Society, Chankya Publications

9. Bose, P.N., History of Hindu Civilisation During the British Rule

10. Desai, I.P., The Craft of Sociology and other Essays, Ajanta Publications Delhi

11. Dumont, Louis, Contributions toIndian Sociology, Vol. 1,7,and 8 ,Mouton&Co.The Hague

12. Gupta, Dipankar, Social Stratification, Oxford University Press, Bombay

13. Marriott, Mckim (Ed), Village India,University of Chicago Press, Chicago

14. Prasad, Narmadeshwar, the Myth of the Caste System, Patna

15. Ross H. Laurence, Perspectives on the Social Order: Readings in sociology McGraw-Hill Book Co., New york

16. Hutton, J.H., Caste in India: Its Nature, Function and Origin, Oxford University Press, Bombay

17. Kapadia, K. M., Sociological bulletin, Vol. XI, September 1962

18. Mukherjee, R.K., The Dynamics of Rural society: A study of the Economic Structure in Bengal Village, Akademic Verlog, Berlin

19. Singh, Yogendra, Modernisation of Indian Tradition, Thomson Press, Delhi

20. Srinivas, M.N., Caste in Modern India and Other essays, Media Promoters and Publishers Bombay

21. BAWS Volume- 7

22. Dutt, N.K., Origin and Growth of Castes in India

23. Rig-Veda Samhita with Sayana's Commentry

24. Yaska's Nirukata

25. Muir,Original Sansktrit texts Weber, The History of Indian Literature

26. Kaegi, Der Rig-Veda

27. Barth, The Religion of India

28. Bloomfield, The Religion of Veda

29. Hopekins, The Religion of India. India ,old and New

30. Journal of the American Oriental Society

31. Oldenberg, Die Religion des Veda; Die Literature des alten Indien

32. Hillebrandt, Vedische Mythologie

33. Max Muller, history of Ancient Sansktrit Literature

34. Chips from a German Workshop

35. Winternitz, the history of Indian Literature

36. Hardy, Die Vedische-brahma-nische Periode der Religion des alten Indiens

37. Macdonell, History of Sanskrit Literature

38. Keith, Religion and Philosophy of the Vedas

39. Wilson, Indian Caste

40. Cambridge History of India I

41. Dutt. N.K., The Aryanisation of India

42. Mitra, R.L., The Indo- Aryans

43. Das, A., rigvedic Culture

44. S. Ayengar, Life in Ancient India in the age og Mantras

45. Sastri, S., evolution of Indian Polity

46. Pargitar, Ancient Indian Historical Tradition

47. Kathaka Samhita

48. Taittiriya Samhita

49. Matriyani Samhita

50. Vajasaneyi samhita

51. Atharvaveda Samhita

52. Aitareya Brahmana

53. Kaushitaki Brahmana

54. Satapatha Brahamana

55. Panchvimsa Brahmana

56. Taittiriya Brahmana

57. Jaiminiya Brahmana

58. Gopatha Brahmana

59. Aitareya Aranyaka

60. Taittiriya Aranyaka

61. Chandyoga Upnishad

62. Brihadarnyaka upnishad

63. Mahabharata

64. Deussen, Die Philosophie der Upanishads

65. Hopkins, Ethics of India

66. Hille Brandt, Ritual-Literature

67. Srauta Sutras- Asvalayana, Katyayana, Sankhayana, Apastamba, Latyayana, Hiranyakesin, Baudhayana

68. Griha Sutras- Asvalayana, Sankhayana, Paraskara, Apasthamba, Gobhila, Manava, Hiranyakesin, Kausika, Khadira, Baudhyana

69. Dharma Sutra- Apastamba, Vasistha,

70. Dharma Sastra- Gautama, Baudhayana, Vishnu

71. Manusamhita

72. Mahabharata

73. Kautilya arthasastra

74. Sparknotes.com/sociology/social-stratification-and-inequality/section

CHAPTER 4

1. BAWS Volume-13

2. Jaiswal Ajeet., Research gate.net/publication/3407627369-Naxalism-and-tribals-in-India

3. BHAGABATI A. C. (2001). Emergent Tribal Identity in North-East India. New Delhi: Concept Publishing Company, 3-9.

4. CENSUS OF INDIA. (2011). Ministry of Home Affairs. Publication Division, New Delhi. 2013, 11-47.

5. JAISWAL, A. (2012). "Tribal Development in North Eastern Part of India: Reality and Constrains". Social Work Chronicle, 1 (2), 68-81.

6. LOYD, ANTHONY (2015). "India's Insurgency". National Geographic (April): 82–94. Retrieved 13 March 2018 https://www.nationalgeographic.com/magazine/2015/04/indiacoal-conflict-minerals-maoist-insurgency/

7. en.wikipedia.org/wiki/Adivasi

8. Encyclopedia Britannica, Adivasi (https://www.britannica.com/topic/Adivasi)

9. Lok Sabha Debates ser.10 Jun 41–42 1995 v.42 no.41-42 (https://books.google.com/?id=EaRXAAAAMAAJ), Lok Sabha Secretariat, Parliament of India, 1995, retrieved 25 November 2008, "...Adivasis are the aborigines of India..."

10. "Supreme Court verdict on harassment of tribal woman" (https://www.thehindu.com/news/resources/Supreme-Court-verdict-on-harassment-of-tribal-woman-pdf-version-full-text/article15519632.ece). thehindu. 11 January 2011. Retrieved 23 April 2021.

11. "Adivasi, n. and adj." OED Online. Oxford University Press, June 2017. Web. 10 September 2017.

12. "PUCL Bulletin, February 2003" (https://web.archive.org/web/20080616184214/http://www.pucl.org/Topics/Dalit-tribal/2003/adivasi.htm). Archived from the original (http://www.pucl.org/Topics/Dalit-tribal/2003/adivasi.htm) on 16 June 2008. Retrieved 27 November 2008.

13. P. 27 Madhya Pradesh: Shajapur By Madhya Pradesh (India)

14. P. 219 Calcutta Review By University of Calcutta, 1964

15. Piya Chatterjee (2001), A Time for Tea: Women, Labor, and Post/colonial Politics on an Indian Plantation (https://books.google.com/?id=Ldw2lX7u-HsC), Duke University Press, ISBN 978-0-8223-2674-8, retrieved 26 November 2008, "...Among the Munda, customary forms of land tenure known as khuntkatti stipulated that land belonged communally to the village, and customary rights of cultivation, branched from corporate ownership. Because of Mughal incursions, non-Jharkhandis began to dominate the agrarian landscape, and the finely wrought system of customary sharing of labor, produce and occupancy began to crumble. The process of dispossession and land alienation, in motion since the mid-eighteenth century, was given impetus by British policies that

established both zamindari and ryotwari systems of land revenue administration. Colonial efforts toward efficient revenue collection hinged on determining legally who had proprietal rights to the land ..."

16. Ulrich van der Heyden; Holger Stoecker (2005), Mission und macht im Wandel politischer Orientierungen: Europäische Missionsgesellschaften in politischen Spannungsfeldern in Afrikaund Asien zwischen 1800 und 1945 (https://books.google.com/?id=N7JfoaVbMGgC), Franz Steiner Verlag, ISBN 978-3-515-08423-9, retrieved 26 November 2008, "... The permanent settlement Act had an adverse effect upon the fate of the Adivasis for, 'the land which the aboriginals had rested from the jungle and cultivated as free men from generation was, by a stroke of pen, declared to be the property of the Raja (king) and the Jagirdars.' The alien became the Zamindars (Landlords) while the sons of the soil got reduced to mere tenants. Now, it was the turn of the Jagirdars-turned-Zamindars who further started leasing out land to the newcomers, who again started encroaching Adivasi land. The land grabbing thus went on unabated. By the year 1832 about 6,411 Adivasi villages were alienated in this process ..."

17. O.P. Ralhan (2002), Encyclopedia of Political Parties (https://books.google.com/?id=_1gQS3LOafAC), Anmol Publications Pvt. Ltd., ISBN 978-81-7488-865-5, retrieved 26 November 2008, "...The Permanent Settlement was 'nothing short of the confiscation of raiyat lands in favor of the zamindars.' ... Marx says '... in Bengal as in Madras and Bombay, under the zamindari as under the ryotwari, the raiyats who form 11/12[ths] of the whole Indian population have been wretchedly pauperised.' To this may be added the inroads made by the Company's Government upon the village community of the tribals (the Santhals, Kols, Khasias etc.)... There was a wholesale destruction of 'the national tradition.' Marx observes: 'England has broken down the entire framework of Indian society ..."

18. Govind Kelkar; Dev Nathan (1991), Gender and Tribe: Women, Land and Forests in Jharkhand (https://books.google. com/?id=cTluAAAAMAAJ), Kali for Women, ISBN 978-1-85649-035-1, retrieved 26 November 2008, "...of the features of the Adivasi land systems. These laws also showed that British colonial rule had passed on to a new stage of exploitation... Forests were the property of the zamindar or the state..." William Wilson Hunter; Hermann Michael Kisch; Andrew Wallace Mackie; Charles James O'Donnell; Herbert Hope Risley (1877), A Statistical Account of Bengal (https://books.google.com/?id=R2MOAAAAQAAJ), Trübner, retrieved 26 November 2008, "... The Kol insurrection of 1831, though, no doubt, only the bursting forth of a fire that had long been smouldering, was fanned into flame by the following episode:- The brother of the Maharaja, who was holder of one of the maintenance grants which comprised Sonpur, a pargana in the southern portion of the estate, gave farms of some of the villages over the heads of the Mankis and Mundas, to certain Muhammadans, Sikhs and others, who has obtained his favour... not only was the Manki dispossessed, but two of his sisters were seduced or ravished by these hated foreigners ... one of them ..., it was said, had abducted and dishonoured the Munda's wife ..."

19. Radhakanta Barik (2006), Land and Caste Politics in Bihar (https:// books.google.com/?id=lGNuAAAAMAAJ), Shipra Publications, ISBN 978-81-7541-305-4, retrieved 26 November 2008, "...As usually the zamindars were the moneylenders, they could pressurize the tenants to concede to high rent..."

20. Sita Venkateswar (2004), Development and Ethnocide: Colonial Practices in the Andaman Islands (https://books.google. com/?id=XFETVExNUYgC), IWGIA, ISBN 978-87-91563-04-1, "...As I have suggested previously, it is probable that some disease was introduced among the coastal groups by Lieutenant Colebrooke and Blair's first settlement in 1789, resulting in a marked reduction of their population. The four years that the British occupied their

initial site on the south-east of South Andaman were sufficient to have decimated the coastal populations of the groups referred to as Jarawa by the Aka-bea-da ..."

21. Luigi Luca Cavalli-Sforza; Francesco Cavalli-Sforza (1995), The Great Human Diasporas: The History of Diversity and Evolution (https://books.google.com/?id=ApuuiwUkEZ0C), Basic Books, ISBN 978-0-201-44231-1, "...Contact with whites, and the British in particular, has virtually destroyed them. Illness, alcohol, and the will of the colonials all played their part; the British governor of the time mentions in his diary that he received instructions to destroy them with alcohol and opium. He succeeded completely with one group. The others reacted violently..."

22. Paramjit S. Judge (1992), Insurrection to Agitation: The Naxalite Movement in Punjab (https://books.google.com/?id=HvYpVtBXw5kC), Popular Prakashan, ISBN 978-81-7154-527-8, retrieved 26 November 2008, "...The Santhal insurrection in 1855–56 was a consequence of the establishment of the permanent Zamindari Settlement introduced by the British in 1793 as a result of which the Santhals had been dispossesed of the land that they had been cultivating for centuries. Zamindars, moneylenders, traders and government officials exploited them ruthlessly. The consequence was a violent revolt by the Santhals which could only be suppressed by the army..."

23. The Indian Journal of Social Work (https://books.google.com/?id=q0c0AAAAIAAJ), v.59, Department of Publications, Tata Institute of Social Sciences, 1956, retrieved 26 November 2008, "...Revolts rose with unfailing regularity and were suppressed with treachery, brute force, tact, cooption and some reforms ..."

24. Roy Moxham (2003), Tea (https://books.google.com/?id=FAiHU5JSYwwC), Carroll & Graf Publishers, ISBN 978-0-7867-1227-4, retrieved 26 November 2008, "...many of the labourers came from Chota Nagpur District ... home to the

Adivasis, the most popular workers with the planters – the '1ˢᵗ class jungley.' As one of the planters, David Crole, observed: 'planters, in a rough and ready way, judge the worth of a coolie by the darkness of the skin.' In the last two decades of the nineteenth century 350,000 coolies went from Chota Nagpur to Assam..."

25. HEUZE, Gérard: Où Va l'Inde Moderne? L'Harmattan, Paris 1993. A. Tirkey: "Evangelization among the Uraons", Indian Missiological Review, June 1997, esp. p. 30-32. Elst 2001

26. Page 63 Tagore Without Illusions by Hitendra Mitra

27. Sameeksha Trust, P. 1229 Economic and Political Weekly

28. P. 4 "Freedom Movement in Khurda" (http://orissagov.nic.in/e-magazine/Orissareview/august-2007/engpdf/Page1-11.pdf) Archived (https://web.archive.org/web/20071129141833/http://orissagov.nic.in/e-magazine/Orissareview/august-2007/engpdf/Page1-11.pdf) 29 November 2007 at the Wayback Machine Dr. Atul Chandra Pradhan

29. P. 111 The Freedom Struggle in Hyderabad: A Connected Account By Hyderabad (India: State)

30. Tribal struggle of Singhbhum

31. S.G. Sardesai (1986), Progress and Conservatism in Ancient India (https://books.google.com/?id=kscNAAAAIAAJ), People's Publishing House, retrieved 25 November 2008, "...The centre of Rig-Vedic religion was the Yajna, the sacrificial fire. ... There is no Atma, no Brahma, no Moksha, no idol worship in the Rig-Veda ..."

32. Shiv Kumar Tiwari (2002), Tribal Roots of Hinduism (https://books.google.com/?id=n0gwfmPFT LgC), Sarup & Sons, ISBN 978-81-7625-299-7, retrieved 12 December 2008

33. Kumar Suresh Singh (1985), Tribal Society in India: An Anthropo-historical Perspective (https://books.google.com/?id=WIAiAAAAMAAJ), Manohar, retrieved 12 December 2008, "...Shiva was a 'tribal deity' to begin with and forest-dwelling

communities, including those who have ceased to be tribals and those who are tribals today ..."

34. "Devoted to God Shiva – An abode for Hindu God Shiva on the Internet" (http://www.shaivam.org/nakanna1.html). Shaivam.org. Retrieved 14 July 2019.

35. "All About Hinduism" (https://web.archive.org/web/20080102233739/http://www.divinelifesociety.org/graphics/ebooks/swami_sivanandaji/downnload/all_about_hinduism.html). Archived from the original (http://www.divinelifesociety.org/graphics/ebooks/swami_sivanandaji/downnload/all_about_hinduism.html) on 2 January 2008. Retrieved 14 July 2019.

36. P. 269 Brāhmanism and Hindūism, Or, Religious Thought and Life in India: As Based on the Veda and Other Sacred Books of the Hindūs (Google eBook) by Sir Monier Monier-Williams

37. "Srivaishnavism" (https://web.archive.org/web/20080504053609/http://www.srivaishnavan.com/tomcat/thiruppa2.htm). Archived from the original (http://www.srivaishnavan.com/tomcat/thiruppa2.htm) on 4 May 2008. Retrieved 14 July 2019.

38. "Archived copy" (https://web.archive.org/web/20070928010508/http://rrtd.nic.in/Birsa.html). Archived from the original (http://rrtd.nic.in/Birsa.html) on 28 September 2007. Retrieved 13 November 2007.

39. "thetribaltribune.com" (https://archive.today/20080502212703/http://www.thetribaltribune.com/V1I2/Birsa.htm). Archive.is. Archived from the original (http://www.thetribaltribune.com/V1I2/Birsa.htm) on 2 May 2008. Retrieved 14 July 2019.

40. "Temples & Legends of Tamilnadu/Srivakuntam – (page3)" (https://web.archive.org/web/20160304103825/http://www.hindubooks.org/temples/tamilnadu/srivaikuntam/page3.htm). Archived from the original (http://www.hindubooks.org/temples/tamilnadu/srivaikuntam/page3.htm) on 4 March 2016. Retrieved 14 July 2019.

41. Thomas Parkhill: The Forest Setting in Hindu Epics.

42. M.S. Golwalkar: Bunch of Thoughts, p.479.

43. JAIN, Girilal: The Hindu Phenomenon. UBSPD, Delhi 1994.

44. Eschmann, Kulke and Tripathi, eds.: Cult of Jagannath, p.97. Elst 2001

45. Mahabharata (I.31–54) (II.37.47; II.44.21) Elst 2001

46. Kautilya: The Arthashastra 9:2:13-20, Penguin edition, p. 685. Elst 2001

47. Bhukya, Bhangya (January 2013). Chatterji, Joya; Peabody, Norbert (eds.). "The Subordination of the Sovereigns: Colonialism and the Gond Rajas in Central India, 1818–1948". Modern Asian Studies. Cambridge University Press. 47 (1): 309. JSTOR 23359786 (https://www.jstor.org/stable/23359786). india: A country study, Federal Research Division –Tribes

48. Anand,S., Annotations, Annihilation of Caste , Navayana Publishing Pvt Ltd. CWMG 68,327

49. Guruswami Mohan, Scroll.in/article/773759/adivasis-india-original-inhabitants_have_suffered_the most_at_its_hands Accessed on 25.04.2021

CHAPTER 5

1. mhmtl: file://://C:\Users\EMPIRE\Downloads. Caste Discrimination-.mhtml.

2. D.B. "Sagar" Bishwakarma, "General Comments of Country Report for the United Nations Convention for Elimination of All Forms of Racial Discrimination," paper prepared by the Academy for Public Upliftment for the Ad Hoc Working Group on the Preparation of NGO Country Report Under the U.N. International Convention on the Elimination of All Forms of Racial Discrimination.

3. Ibid.

4. Rajendra Kalidas Wimala Goonesekere, "Prevention of Discrimination and Protection of Indigenous Peoples and Minorities" (New York: United Nations, 2001) E/CN.4/Sub. 2/2001/16, para. 38

5. "Nepal Prohibits Bias Against Untouchable Caste," The New York Times, August 17, 2001.

6. Committee on the Elimination of Racial Discrimination, "Fourteenth Periodic Reports of States Parties Due in 1996: India," CERD/C/299/Add.3, para. 7, April 29, 1996.

7. Committee on the Elimination of Racial Discrimination, "Fourteenth Report of States Parties Due in 1998: Nepal," CERD/C/337/Add.4, para. 22, May 12, 1999.

8. Ibid., para. 38.

9. Goonesekere, "Prevention of Discrimination" (New York: United Nations, 2001), E/CN.4/Sub. 2/2001/16, paras. 28-29.

10. In research conducted by Human Rights Watch in Sri Lanka in 1999, displaced members of the Kuravar minority, a non-Tamil tribal group, complained that their Tamil neighbors were preventing them from using a village water supply because they were viewed as low caste or "untouchable." Sri Lankan Tamil internally displaced persons (IDPs) in Trincomalee also complained when they were forced to live in close proximity to Tamils of Indian origin, whom they considered lower caste. Human Rights Watch interviews, April 1999.

11. Oddvar Hollup, "Caste Identity and Cultural Continuity Among Tamil plantation workers in Sri Lanka," Journal of Asian and African studies, vol. 28, nos. 1-2 (1993), pp. 79-81.

12. Jerome Njikwulimchukwu Okafor, The Challenge of Osu Caste System to the Igbo Christians (Onitsha: Veritas Printing and Publishing, 1993), p. 33.

13. Ian Neary, "Burakumin in Contemporary Japan" in Michael Weiner (ed.) Japan's Minorities: The Illusion of Homogeneity (London: Routledge, 1997), p. 55.

14. International Movement Against All Forms of Discrimination and Racism and Buraku Liberation League and Buraku Liberation and Human Rights Research Institute, "Reality of Buraku Discrimination in Japan: History, Situation, Challenge," February 2001, pp. 7-8.

15. Ibid., p. 10.

16. "Kyoto," Encyclopedia Britannica Online, http://members. eb.com/bol/topic?eu=109591&sctn=4, (accessed July 18, 2001).

17. Leslie D. Alldritt, "The Burakumin: The Complicity of Japanese Buddhism in Oppression and an Opportunity for Liberation," Journal of Buddhist Ethics, vol. 7 (2000), available at http://jbe. la.psu.edu/7/alldritt001.html (accessed March 28, 2001).

18. Yuka Ishikawa, "Rights Activists and Rights Violations: The Burakumin Case in Japan," paper prepared by the Buraku Liberation League for the Global Conference Against Racism and Caste-Based Discrimination, New Delhi, India, March 1-4, 2001, available at http://www.imadr.org/tokyo/ishikawareport.html (accessed May 21, 2001).

19. Ishikawa, "Rights Activists and Rights Violations."

20. Buraku Liberation and Human Rights Research Institute and Buraku Liberation League, Buraku People.

21. http://www.geocities.com/jbenhill/thesisChap2.html (accessed July 26, 2001).

22. "Bangladesh Dalit Hindus Fight for Jobs and Homes," Indian Express, September 20, 2000.

23. Ibid.

24. P.P. Sivapragasam, "Indian Origin Tamils in Sri Lanka: An Oppressed People" (paper prepared by the National Campaign on Dalit Human Rights for the Global Conference Against Racism and Caste-Based Discrimination/Occupation and Descent Based Discrimination Against Dalits, New Delhi, India March 1-4, 2001).

25. Goonesekere, "Prevention of Discrimination" (New York: United Nations, 2001) E/CN.4/Sub. 2/2001/16, para. 32

26. Ibid.

27. Ibid., para. 36.

28. Anti-Slavery International, "Persistence of slavery in Mauritania and repression of anti-slavery activists," oral statement to U.N. Subcommission on Prevention of Discrimination and Protection of Minorities (delivered by Abdel Nasser Ould Othman Sid' Ahmed, translated from French original) August 1998.

29. Human Rights Watch, letter to John Rosenbaum, Assistant USTR for Trade and Development, Office of the U.S. Trade Representative, May 14, 1999. See also Kevin Bales, Disposable People: New Slavery in the Global Economy (Berkeley: University of California Press, 1999).

30. Buraku Liberation League and Buraku Liberation and Human Rights Research Institute, Reality of Discriminated-Against Buraku People in Japan and the Challenge Aiming for the Elimination of Discrimination (Japan: Buraku Liberation and Human Rights Research Institute, 2001), p. 60.

31. Buraku Liberation and Human Rights Research Institute and Buraku Liberation League, "Buraku People," (Japan: Discrimination Against Buraku People).

32. ohchr.org/en/hrbodies/hrc/pages/home.aspx

33. ohchr.org/Documents/ HR bodies/ HR Council/ Regular session II/A-HRC-II-CRP-3.pdf

34. un.org/en/about –us/Universal Declaration-of human-rights

35. un.org/en/about-us/history-of-the-un

36. Asia Dalits Rights Forum, Discrimination Based on Work and Descent and Untouchability

37. Alternative Report to the UN Committee on the Elimination of Racial Discrimination in review of the 21-23 periodic reports of the United Kingdom- Caste-Based discrimination in UK

38. ISDN briefing paper (2014) – Caste Discrimination in UK

39. Roma people in Europe in the 21st century: violence, exclusion and insecurity A European Association for the defence of Human Rights Report.

40. The Roma People in Europe- Peace Research, Richardson Institution,(2014).

CHAPTER 6

1. Ambedkar, B.R., BAWS, Vol.1

2. C:/users/Dell/Desktop/Jyotirao/ Wikipedia.html

3. en.wikipedia.org/wiki/Jyotirao Phule

4. Phule, Jotirao (1991). Selections: Collected Works of Mahatma Jotirao Phule Vol II (http://booksdescr.org/ads. php?md5=d0b5f4caf0917b30dbae350f0abd3946).   Mumbai: Government of Maharashtra. pp. xv.

5. 15. Phule, Jotirao (1991). Selections: Collected Works of Mahatma Jotirao Phule Vol II (http://booksdescr.org/ads. php?md5=d0b5f4caf0917b30dbae350f0abd3946).   Mumbai: Government of Maharashtra. pp. xvi.

6. O'Hanlon (2002), p. 135 sfnp error: multiple targets (2×): CITEREFO'Hanlon2002 (help)

7. Bhadru, G. (2002). "Contribution of Shatyashodhak Samaj to the Low Caste Protest Movement

8. in 19th Century". Proceedings of the Indian History Congress. 63: 845–854. JSTOR 44158153 (https://www.jstor.org/stable/44158153).

9. "Life & Work of Mahatma Jotira" (https://web.archive.org/web/20090311014003/http://www.unipune.ernet.in/chairs/mahatmaphule/lifework.htm). University of Pune. Archived from the original (http://www.unipune.ernet.in/chairs/mahatmaphule/lifework.htm) on 11 March 2009. International Journal of Humanities and social sciences Invention(IJHSSI)ISSN(online) 2319-7714 www.ijhssi.org//volume 8issue 03 serve-in March 2019/1 P-43-50

10. en.wikipedia.org/wiki/Ambedkar

11. "Dr. Ambedkar" (https://web.archive.org/web/20121008195805/http://www.ncdhr.org.in/ncdhr/general-info-misc-pages/dr-ambedkar). National Campaign on Dalit Human Rights. Archived from the original (http://www.ncdhr.org.in/ncdhr/general-info-misc-pages/dr-ambedkar) on 8 October 2012. Retrieved 12 January 2012.

12. Kumar, Aishwary. "The Lies Of Manu" (http://www.outlookindia.com/article/The-Lies-Of-Manu/2 81937). outlookindia.com. Archived (https://web.archive.org/web/20151018233954/http://www.outlookindia.com/article/the-lies-of-manu/281937) from the original on 18 October 2015.

13. "Annihilating caste" (http://www.frontline.in/static/html/fl2815/stories/20110729281509500.htm).frontline.in. Archived (https://web.archive.org/web/20140528172120/http://www.frontline.in/static/html/fl2815/stories/20110729281509500.htm) from the original on 28 May 2014.

14. en.wikipedia.org/wiki/Narayana_Guru

15. "Narayana Guru, 1856-1928" (https://id.loc.gov/authorities/names/n82142354.html). LC Name Authority File. Library of Congress. Retrieved 18 March 2021.

16. Pullapilly, Cyriac K. (1976). "The Izhavas of Kerala and their Historic Struggle for Acceptance in the Hindu Society". In Smith, Bardwell L. (ed.). Religion and social conflict in South Asia (https://books.google.com/books?id=xNAI9F8IBOgC). International studies in sociology and social anthropology. 22. BRILL. pp. 24–46. ISBN 978-90-04-04510-1.

17. "125 years of Aruvipuram Pratishta" (http://www.newindianexpress.com/cities/chennai/2013/aug/22/125-years-of-Aruvipuram-Pratishta-509120.html). The New Indian Express. Retrieved 1 April 2019.

18. "Sree Narayana Guru in a new light" (https://web.archive.org/web/20131113133024/http://newindianexpress.com/cities/kochi/article167942.ece?service=print). 13 November 2013. Archived from the original (http://newindianexpress.com/cities/kochi/article167942.ece?service=print) on 13 November 2013. Retrieved 1 April 2019.

19. "Guru-varsham 150: The year of Sree Narayana Guru" (https://www.rediff.com/news/2004/aug/30rajeev.htm). www.rediff.com. Retrieved 1 April 2019.
See also
Notes
References

20. Staff Reporter (7 October 2009). "Kerala recommends national prayer song to Centre" (https://www.thehindu.com/news/national/kerala/Kerala-recommends-national-prayer-song-to-Centre/article16885319.ece). The Hindu. Retrieved 1 April 2019.

21. "Writings of Sree Narayana Guru" (https://www.sndp.org/html/writings.html). www.sndp.org. Retrieved 1 April 2019.

22. Diane P. Mines; Sarah Lamb; Sarah E. Lamb (2010). Everyday Life in South Asia (https://books.google.com/books?id=828fOvb61wIC&pg=PA209). Indiana University Press. pp. 209–.ISBN 978-0-253-35473-0.R. Raman Nair; L. Sulochana

Devi (2010). Chattampi Swami: An Intellectual Biography-1 (https:// books.google.com/books?id=K-JRfipEdV0C&pg=PA189). South Indian Studies. pp. 189–.ISBN 978-81-905928-2-6.

23. Bardwell L. Smith (1976). Religion and Social Conflict in South Asia (https://books.google.com/ books?id=xNAI9F8IBOgC&pg=PA42). BRILL. pp. 42–. ISBN 90-04-04510-4.

24. Staff Reporter (8 March 2016). "All-religion meet begins at Aluva" (https://www.thehindu.com/news/cities/Kochi/allreligion-meet-begins-at-aluva/article8325913.ece). The Hindu. Retrieved 1 April 2019.

25. en.wikipedia.org/wiki/Dalit-Panthers

26. Rajawat, p. 325

27. Rajawat, Mamta (2004). Encyclopedia of Dalits in India, Volume 1 (https://books.google. com/?id=oXNQvgAACAAJ&dq=Encyclopedia+of+Dalits+in+ In+mamta). Anmol Publications. p. 325. ISBN 978-81-261-2084-0.

28. Michael, S. M. (2007). Dalits in modern India: vision and values (https://books.google.com/book s?id=xnyo1xPNwxwC&pg=PA172). SAGE. p. 173. ISBN 978-0-7619-3571-1. Retrieved 9 January 2010.

29. "Dalit Panthers: Another View". Economic and Political Weekly. 9 (18): 715–716. 1974. ISSN 0012-9976 (https://www.worldcat.org/issn/0012-9976). JSTOR 41497050 (https://www.jstor.org/stable/41497050).

30. "The last Panther" (https://www.mid-day.com/articles/the-last-panther/21386193). mid-day. 21 July 2019. Retrieved 8 August 2019.

31. Satyanarayana and Tharu (2013). The Exercise of Freedom: An Introduction to Dalit Writing. New Delhi: Navayana. p. 55. ISBN 978-8-18905-961-3.

32. en.wikipedia.org/wiki/BAMCEF

33. Jaffrelot 2010, p. 535.

34. en.wikipedia.org/wiki/Kanshi-Ram

35. Narayan, Badri (11 May 2012). "Ambedkar and Kanshi Ram – so alike, yet so different" (http://www.thehindu.com/opinion/op-ed/ambedkar-and-kanshi-ram-so-alike-yet-so-different/article3405293.ece). The Hindu. Retrieved 15 May 2016.

36. Waghmore, Suryakant. Civility against Caste: Dalit Politics and Citizenship in Western India (https://books.google.com/books?id=PPenAwAAQBAJ&pg=PA40). Sage. p. 40.

37. Bagchi, Suvojit (17 November 2013). "Chhattisgarh polls: Towards a photo finish" (https://www.thehindu.com/news/national/other-states/chhattisgarh-polls-towards-a-photo-finish/article5359312.ece). The Hindu. ISSN 0971-751X (https://www.worldcat.org/issn/0971-751X). Retrieved 9 August 2018.

38. Rawat, Ramnarayan (23 October 2006). "The Dalit Chanakya" (http://www.outlookindia.com/article.aspx?232896). Outlook. Retrieved 16 October 2016.

39. Sherring, M.A., Hindu Tribes and Castes, Trübner & Co., London

40. en.wikipedia.org/wiki/Ramanuj

41. en.wikipedia.org/wiki/Bhakti Poets

42. Schomer & McLeod (1987), p. 1.

43. https://www.indiatoday.in/education-today/gk-current-affairs/story/-crashcourse-cbse-class-12-history-bhakti-movement-s-emergence-and-influence-1438286-2019-01-24 (https://www.indiatoday.in/education-today/gk-current-affairs/story/-crashcourse-cbse-class-12-history-bhakti-movement-s-emergence-and-influence-1438286-2019-01-24). Missing or empty |title= (help)

44. Schomer & McLeod (1987), pp. 1-2.
    See also
    Notes
    References

45. Lance Nelson (2007), An Introductory Dictionary of Theology and Religious Studies (Editors: Orlando O. Espín, James B. Nickoloff), Liturgical Press, ISBN 978-0814658567, pages 562-563

46. SS Kumar (2010), Bhakti – the Yoga of Love, LIT Verlag Münster, ISBN 978-3643501301, pages 35-36

47. Wendy Doniger (2009), "Bhakti" (http://www.britannica.com/EBchecked/topic/63933/bhakti), Encyclopædia Britannica

48. "The Four Denominations of Hinduism" (http://www.himalayanacademy.com/readlearn/basics/four-sects). Himalayan Academy. 2013.

49. Johar, Surinder (1999). Guru Gobind Singh: A Multi-faceted Personality. MD Publications. p. 89. ISBN 978-8-175-33093-1.

50. Schomer & McLeod (1987), p. 2.

51. Christian Novetzke (2007). "Bhakti and Its Public". International Journal of Hindu Studies. 11 (3): 255–272. doi:10.1007/s11407-008-9049-9 (https://doi.org/10.1007%2Fs11407-008-9049-9). JSTOR 25691067 (https://www.jstor.org/stable/25691067). S2CID 144065168 (https://api.semanticscholar.org/CorpusID:144065168).

52. Pechilis Prentiss (2014), pp. 10-16.

53. Pechilis Prentiss (2014), pp. 15-16.

54. Catherine Robinson (2005), Interpretations of the Bhagavad-Gita and Images of the Hindu Tradition, Routledge, ISBN 978-0415346719, pages 28-30

55. Pechilis Prentiss (2014), pp. 26-32, 217-218.

56. Pechilis Prentiss, Karen (1999). The Embodiment of Bhakti. US: Oxford University Press. p. 24. ISBN 978-0-19-512813-0.

57. Werner, Karel (1993). Love Divine: studies in bhakti and devotional mysticism. Routledge. p. 168. ISBN 978-0-7007-0235-0.

58. Monier Monier-Williams, Monier-Williams Sanskrit English Dictionary, Motilal Banarsidass, page 743

59. bhakti (http://spokensanskrit.de/index. php?tinput=bhakti&direction=SE&script=HK&link=yes&b eginning=0) Sanskrit English Dictionary, University of Koeln, Germany

60. Pechilis Prentiss (2014), pp. 19-21.

61. Pechilis Prentiss (2014), p. 3.

62. Madeleine Biardeau (1994), Hinduism: The Anthropology of a Civilisation (Original: French), Oxford University Press, ISBN 978-0195633894 (English Translation by Richard Nice), pages 89-91

63. Shvetashvatara Upanishad 6.23 (https://sa.wikisource.org/ wiki/तातरोप नषद् Wikisource

64. Paul Carus, The Monist (https://books.google.com/ books?id=96sLAAAAIAAJ) at Google Books, pages 514-515

65. Paul Deussen, Sixty Upanishads of the Veda, Volume 1, Motilal Banarsidass, ISBN 978-8120814684, page 326

66. Max Muller, Shvetashvatara Upanishad (https://archive.org/ stream/upanishads02ml#page/266/mode/2up), The Upanishads, Part II, Oxford University Press, page 267

67. WN Brown (1970), Man in the Universe: Some Continuities in Indian Thought, University of

68. California Press, ISBN 978-0520017498, pages 38-39

69. Paul Deussen, Sixty Upanishads of the Veda, Volume 1, Motilal Banarsidass, ISBN 978-8120814684, pages 301-304

70. Max Muller, The Shvetashvatara Upanishad (https://archive.org/stream/upanishads02ml#page/n33/mode/2up), Oxford University Press, pages xxxii – xlii Max Muller, The Shvetashvatara Upanishad (https://archive.org/stream/upanishads02ml#page/n33/mode/2up), Oxford University Press, pages xxxiv and xxxvii

71. D Srinivasan (1997), Many Heads, Arms, and Eyes, Brill, ISBN 978-9004107588, pages 96-97 and Chapter 9

72. Lee Siegel (October 1978). "Commentary: Theism in Indian Thought". Philosophy East and West. 28 (4): 419–423. doi:10.2307/1398646 (https://doi.org/10.2307%2F1398646). JSTOR 1398646 (https://www.jstor.org/stable/1398646).

73. R Tsuchida (1985). "Some Remarks on the Text of the Svetasvatara-Upanisad". Journal of Indian and Buddhist Studies (印度學佛教學研究). 34 (1): 460–468. "The Svetasvatara-Upanisad occupies a highly unique position among Vedic Upanisads as a testimony of the meditative and monistic Rudra-cult combined with Samkhya-Yoga doctrines."

74. M. Hiriyanna (2000), The Essentials of Indian Philosophy, Motilal Banarsidass, ISBN 978-8120813304, pages 32-36

75. Fowler (2012), see Foreword.

76. Minor, Robert Neil (1986). Modern Indian Interpreters of the Bhagavadgita (https://books.google.com/books?id=Ku2DGm20WWUC&pg=PA3). SUNY Press. p. 3. ISBN 978-0-88706-297-1.

77. Glucklich, Ariel (2008). The Strides of Vishnu (https://books.google.com/books?id=KtLScrjrWiAC&pg=PA104). Oxford University Press. p. 104. ISBN 978-0-19-531405-2.

78. Jacobsen, Knut A., ed. (2005). Theory And Practice of Yoga: Essays in Honour of Gerald James Larson. Brill Academic Publishers. p. 351. ISBN 90-04-14757-8.

79. Christopher Key Chapple (Editor) and Winthrop Sargeant (Translator), The Bhagavad Gita: Twenty-fifth–Anniversary Edition, State University of New York Press, ISBN 978-1438428420, pages 302-303, 318

80. Bary, William Theodore De; Stephen N Hay (1988). "Hinduism" (https://books.google.com/books?id=PqzFZNF2RxgC&pg=PA330). Sources of Indian Tradition. Motilal Banarsidass. p. 330. ISBN 978-81-208-0467-8.

81. Georg Feuerstein; Ken Wilber (2002). The Yoga Tradition (https://books.google.com/books?id=Yy5s2EHXFwAC&pg=PA55). Motilal Banarsidass. p. 55. ISBN 978-81-208-1923-8.

82. Swami Vivekananda (2006). "Bhakti Yoga" (https://books.google.com/books?id=usBhrZcnJ78C&pg=PA212). In Amiya P Sen (ed.). The indispensable Vivekananda. Orient Blackswan.p. 212. ISBN 978-81-7824-130-2.

83. SM Pandey (1965). "Mīrābāī and Her Contributions to the Bhakti Movement". History of Religions. 5 (1): 54–73. doi:10.1086/462514 (https://doi.org/10.1086%2F462514). JSTOR 1061803 (https://www.jstor.org/stable/1061803). S2CID 162398500 (https://api.semanticscholar.org/CorpusID:162398500).

84. Embree, Ainslie Thomas; Stephen N. Hay; William Theodore De Bary (1988). Sources of Indian Tradition. Columbia University Press. p. 342. ISBN 978-0-231-06651-8.

85. Flood, Gavin (1996). An Introduction to Hinduism (https://archive.org/details/introductiontohi0000floo). Cambridge University Press. pp. 131 (https://archive.org/details/introductiontohi0000floo/page/131). ISBN 978-0-521-43878-0.

86. Olson, Carl (2007). The many colors of Hinduism: a thematic-historical introduction. Rutgers University Press. p. 231. ISBN 978-0-8135-4068-9.

87. Sheridan, Daniel (1986). The Advaitic Theism of the Bhagavata Purana. Columbia, Mo: South Asia Books. ISBN 81-208-0179-2.

88. J. A. B. van Buitenen (1996). "The Archaism of the Bhāgavata Purāṇa". In S.S. Shashi (ed.). Encyclopedia Indica. pp. 28–45. ISBN 978-81-7041-859-7.

89. Pechilis Prentiss (2014), pp. 17-18.

90. Note: The earliest arrival dates are contested by scholars. They range from 7th to 9th century, with Muslim traders settling in coastal regions of Indian peninsula, to Muslims seeking asylum in Tamil Nadu, to raids in northwest India by Muhammad bin Qasim. See: Annemarie Schimmel (1997), Islam in the Indian subcontinent, Brill Academic, ISBN 978-9004061170, pages 3-7; Andre Wink (2004), Al-Hind: the Making of the Indo-Islamic World, Brill Academic Publishers, ISBN 90-04-09249-8

91. Karen Pechelis (2011), "Bhakti Traditions", in The Continuum Companion to Hindu Studies (Editors: Jessica Frazier, Gavin Flood), Bloomsbury, ISBN 978-0826499660, pages 107-121

92. Hawley (2015), pp. 39-61.

93. Rekha Pande (2014), Divine Sounds from the Heart—Singing Unfettered in their Own Voices, Cambridge UK, ISBN 978-1443825252, page 25

94. Vasudha Narayanan (1994), The Vernacular Veda: Revelation, Recitation, and Ritual, The University of South Carolina Press, ISBN 978-0872499652, page 84

95. Gavin Flood (2003). The Blackwell companion to Hinduism. Wiley-Blackwell. p. 185. ISBN 978-0-631-21535-6.

96. Stephen Neill (2002), A history of Christianity in India, 1707-1858, Cambridge University Press, ISBN 978-0-521-89332-9, page 412

97. Mary Kelting (2001), Singing to the Jinas: Jain laywomen, Maṇḍaḷ singing, and the negotiations of Jain devotion, Oxford University Press, page 87, ISBN 978-0-19-514011-8

98. Klaus G Witz (1998), The Supreme Wisdom of the Upaniṣads: An Introduction, Motilal Banarsidass, ISBN 978-8120815735, page 10

99. Guy Beck (2011), Sonic Liturgy: Ritual and Music in Hindu Tradition, The University of South Carolina Press, ISBN 978-1611170375, Chapters 3 and 4

100. David Kinsley (1979), The Divine Player: A Study of Kṛṣṇa Līlā, Motilal Banarsidass, ISBN 978-0896840195, pages 190-204

101. Richard Kieckhefer and George Bond (1990), Sainthood: Its Manifestations in World Religions, University of California Press, ISBN 978-0520071896, pages 116-122

102. Hawley (2015), pp. 304-310.

103. Lorenzen (1995), pp. 182-199.

104. Mukherjee, Sujit (1998). A dictionary of Indian literature. Hyderabad: Orient Longman. ISBN 81-250-1453-5. OCLC 42718918 (https://www.worldcat.org/oclc/42718918).

105. Peasants and Monks in British India, University of California Press, ISBN 978-0520200616, pages 2–3, 53-81

106. Rupert Snell (1991), The Hindi Classical Tradition: A Braj Bhāṣā Reader, Routledge, ISBN 978-0728601758, pages 39-40

107. Rachel McDermott (2001), Singing to the Goddess: Poems to Kālī and Umā from Bengal, Oxford University Press, ISBN 978-0195134346, pages 8-9

108. Maheswar Neog (1995), Early History of the Vaiṣṇava Faith and Movement in Assam: Śaṅkaradeva and his times, Motilal Banarsidass, ISBN 978-8120800076, pages 1-4

109. Learning History Civis Standard Seven (https://books.google.com/books?id=uZxdatjyWkEC&pg=PA29). Jeevandeep Prakashan Pvt Ltd. p. 30. GGKEY:CYCRSZJDF4J.

110. Rekha Pande (13 September 2010). Divine Sounds from the Heart—Singing Unfettered in their Own Voices: The Bhakti

Movement and its Women Saints (12th to 17th Century) (https://books.google.com/books?id=mYEnBwAAQBAJ&pg=PA162). Cambridge Scholars Publishing. pp. 162–163. ISBN 978-1-4438-2525-2.

111. Schomer & McLeod (1987).

112. Axel Michaels (2003), Hinduism: Past and Present, Princeton University Press, ISBN 978-0691089539, pages 62-65

113. Pechilis Prentiss (2014), p. 21.

114. Fowler (2012), pp. xxvii-xxxiv.

115. Fowler (2012), pp. 207-211.

116. Jessica Frazier and Gavin Flood (2011), The Continuum Companion to Hindu Studies, Bloomsbury Academic, ISBN 978-0826499660, pages 113-115

117. David Lorenzen (1996), Praises to a Formless God: Nirguni Texts from North India, State University of New York Press, ISBN 978-0791428054, page 2

118. Iwao (1988), pp. 184-185

119. Peter van der Veer (1987). "Taming the Ascetic: Devotionalism in a Hindu Monastic Order". Man. New Series. 22 (4): 680–695.

120. Hawley (2015), pp. 338-339.

121. Schomer & McLeod (1987), pp. 154-155.

122. Nirmal Dass (2000), Songs of the Saints from the Adi Granth, State University of New York Press, ISBN 978-0791446836, pages 181-184

123. A term in Shaiva Hindu religiosity, referring to an individual who is always on the go, seeking, learning; See: Winnand Callewaert (2000), The Hagiographies of Anantadas: The Bhakti Poets of North India, Routledge, ISBN 978-0700713318, page 292

124. Winnand Callewaert (2000), The Hagiographies of Anantadas: The Bhakti Poets of North India, Routledge, ISBN 978-0700713318, page 292

125. Venketesh Kartik., C:/Users/Dell/Desktop/references/a-brief-history-of –theBhakti movement

Chapter 7

1. Sherring, M.a., Hindu and Tribes of Castes Volume 3, Trübner & Co., London

2. Ambedkar, B.R., BAWS Vol .1

3. The Doctor and the saint by Arundhati Roy

4. Gupta. O.P., http://sify.com/news/othernews/fullstory.php?id=13167991

5. JT- Origin Of Caste in India

6. Ambedkar, B.R., BAWS Vol. 7

7. Niwar Sanjeev., Dalits of Hindustan

8. Columbia.edu/its/mealac/Prichett/00ambedkar/timeline/graphics/text-Gandhi-1936- Bhangi.pdfNcdhr.org.in/wp-content/uploads/2019/05/Discrimination-based–on-work-descent-and-untouchability-pdf

Chapter 8

1. BAWS Vol. 17 (1)